SUBRAMANIA BHARATI

VA. RA., born Varadarajan Ramaswamy in 1889 in Thingalur, Tamil Nadu, was a writer and social activist who opposed British rule from a young age and was imprisoned in 1930 for joining the Salt March. His novels *Sundari* and *Vijayam* were ahead of their time in advocating women's rights, and his vivid portrayals of ordinary people influenced later writers to focus on marginalized communities. As editor of *Manikodi*, he helped shape modern Tamil literature, and his biography of Subramania Bharati is considered a classic. He married Bhuvaneswari in 1936 while working in Colombo, lived with a progressive, rebellious spirit, and died in 1951 at the age of sixty-two.

AMSHAN KUMAR is a filmmaker and a writer. He has made several documentaries on art, theatre, music, literature and environment. His documentary on Yazhpanam Thedchanamoorthy, a legendary Thavil player, won him a National Award. His two feature films in Tamil, *Oruthi* and *Manusangada*, participated in many film festivals and won awards. He has written many books on films and literature. He has also translated books from Tamil to English and English to Tamil. He was given Bharati Pasarai Award for the year 2023. He conducts workshops on filmmaking and film appreciation. His writings appear in Tamil and English regularly in magazines. He lives in Chennai.

MISSION STATEMENT

This is an initiative of the Tamil Nadu Textbook and Educational Services Corporation (TNTB & ESC) under the aegis of one of the announcements for the year 2023-24, by Honourable Minister for School Education Thiru. Anbil Mahesh Poyyamozhi titled the Translation of Rare and Nationalised Literary Tamil Works into English. These ventures are to be undertaken as either independent or joint publications with collaborating English language publishers.

Members, Academic Advisory Committee (Translation)

1. Dr. R. Balakrishnan, IAS, Researcher and Writer
2. Thiru. S. Ramakrishnan, Writer
3. Thiru. S. Madasamy, Educationist

Project Execution Team

1. Thiru. Dindigul I. Leoni, Chairperson, TNTB & ESC
2. Dr. M. Aarthi. IAS, Managing Director, TNTB & ESC
3. Dr. C. Usha Rani, Member Secretary, TNTB & ESC
4. Ms S. Thenmozhi, Deputy Director (Publications), TNTB & ESC
5. Dr. T.S. Saravanan, Honorary Advisor (Translations), TNTB & ESC
6. Dr. P. Saravanan, Assistant Director (Publications), TNTB & ESC
7. Thiru. M. Appanasamy, Consultant, TNTB & ESC
8. Tmt. Mini Krishnan, Co-ordinating Editor, TNTB & ESC

The publisher has no objection to this English translation being used to facilitate transfers into other languages.

SUBRAMANIA BHARATI

AN INTIMATE PORTRAIT OF A REVOLUTIONARY POET

VA. RA.

Translated from the Tamil
and with an introduction and notes
by

AMSHAN KUMAR

hachette INDIA

TAMIL NADU TEXTBOOK AND EDUCATIONAL SERVICES CORPORATION
LEARN THOROUGHLY

Subramania Bharati is the translation of *Mahakavi Bharatiyar*, originally written in Tamil by Va. Ra. It was first serialized in *Gandhi* magazine between 1933–34, and subsequently revised and published as a book by Sakthi Kariyalayam in 1944.

First English translation published in 2021 by Sol Aer Pathippagam

This edition published in 2026 by Hachette India
(Registered name: Hachette Book Publishing India Pvt. Ltd)
An Hachette UK company
www.hachetteindia.com

1

Amshan Kumar's photograph by Rajeev Anand

Cover design and illustration by Harshavardhan Behura

Hardback ISBN 978-93-5731-849-5
Paperback ISBN 978-93-5731-920-1
eBook ISBN 978-93-5731-545-6

Hachette Book Publishing India Pvt. Ltd
4th & 5th Floors, Corporate Centre,
Plot No. 94, Sector 44, Gurugram 122003, India

Typeset in Calluna 11.2/16.5 by R. Ajith Kumar, New Delhi

Printed and bound in India
by Manipal Technologies Limited

MIX
Paper | Supporting responsible forestry
FSC™ C043100

For Thara

Contents

Introduction

I

LIKE SEVERAL INCIDENTS THAT TOOK PLACE IN HIS eventful life, Subramania Bharati's first decisive encounter with the British India police had also a dash of theatricality to it. The story goes that he was climbing down the staircase of the weekly *India*'s office where he was working, in Broadway in Chennai, that overlooked the Bay of Bengal. While doing so, in all probability he was singing, as was his wont, while involuntarily engaged in any activity. Halfway down the stairs, he saw a policeman ascending. Bharati stopped as the policeman held out an arrest warrant. He read it quickly and told the policeman to seek the editor in the office upstairs. The warrant had been issued to arrest the editor of *India* for publishing treasonous articles. As the policeman went up to arrest M. Srinivasan Iyengar, *India*'s official editor, Bharati reached the ground and could have as well cast one last look at the office above, for he knew he would never ever return to it.[1]

At that time, important political leaders in India were being arrested under the British rule, and it was strongly suspected that the government was gunning for Bharati for some time.[2] As luck would have it, he escaped its immediate snare, for he was in fact looking after all the editorial work in *India* unofficially. But he wanted to act fast, lest he might not be lucky once again when another warrant could be issued for his arrest at any time. Acting upon the advice of his well-wishers, he left India for Puducherry, then a French colony, about two hundred kilometres away from Chennai by train. Thus began the decade-long self-imposed exile of Subramania Bharati, one of the great poets of our time.

Bharati arrived in Puducherry in the first week of September 1908. For a few days, he did not know where he would find his shelter in the hitherto unfamiliar territory. But everything fell into place in the next few days. His friends S.N. Thirumalachariar, the founder of *India* magazine, and Mandayam Srinivasachariar also arrived there shortly.

Puducherry was new to him, but *India* weekly had its subscribers there. With the support of his friends, he resumed its publication the very next month he landed there. *India*'s second and final innings ended two years later because its copies were not allowed to reach subscribers in India.[3] There was nothing unusual in its closure for Bharati, who had worked as a journalist in several periodicals during his life and had met with similar circumstances: except *Swadesamitran*, where he was initiated into journalism and where he had last worked, all the others had only short periods of existence before they folded up once and for all.

Nationalist and philosopher Aurobindo Ghose and the Tamil writer and revolutionary Va.Ve.Su. Iyer reached Puducherry in the next few years, and Bharati immediately established contact with them. Bharati had by then acquired other friends and also disciples. The small circle began to enlarge even as the surveillance of the secret police increased and his activities were keenly watched. When the Collector of Tirunelveli and District Magistrate, Robert William d'Escourt Ashe, was shot dead by a freedom fighter named Vanchinathan at Maniyachi railway station in June 1911, the British government thought Bharati had a hand in it. Copies of his books *Kanavu* and *Aaril Oru Pangu* found in the suspect's custody were 'proof' enough to establish suspicion.

It was at this juncture in June 1911 when Va. Ra. entered Puducherry from British India. Kodiyalam V. Rangasamy Iyengar, a member of the British Council of State in Delhi, was secretly helping the patriots. Va. Ra. was sent as his envoy to meet Aurobindo in Puducherry. Only a year before, Aurobindo had reached the French colony after he was acquitted in the Alipore Bomb case, for which he had spent a year in jail. But the ordeals of persecution were not over and they led him to flee Calcutta (now Kolkata). Va. Ra. did not know much about Aurobindo before he met him. But he had read Bharati's patriotic songs and also knew a few other details about him. Perhaps that acquaintance led him to go straight to Bharati instead of his assigned destination. Also, for many to reach Aurobindo in Puducherry, Bharati was the favoured signpost.

Va. Ra. met Aurobindo on the very first day of his arrival, thanks to Bharati, but he extended his stay in Puducherry which went on until 21 January 1914. Va. Ra. wrote his memoir of Bharati, serially in *Gandhi*, a Tamil magazine, in 1933–34, that was published as a book *Mahakavi Bharatiyar* in 1944.[4] Besides recording his meetings with Bharati, Va. Ra. traversed back and forth to give the readers a fair account of Bharati's life in his biography. On a few occasions, some of them had come from Bharati himself. For instance, his longing for his mother since he lost her when he was barely five years old. Va. Ra.'s accounts, in the main, do not contradict the accounts given by Bharati's contemporaries and they reveal far more than any other biography of him. It occupies a place no other account of Bharati can ever reach, since there cannot be anyone who can equal Va. Ra. in his passionate admiration of him both as a man and as a poet.

Va. Ra. focused intently on Bharati to the exclusion of Bharati's family. There is no significant account of Bharati's wife Chellammal, and their two daughters, Thangammal and Sakunthala. Va. Ra., besides portraying Bharati, addresses chiefly the existential issues he confronted as a refugee and the studies he conducted on Bharati after his demise.

The first meeting of Va. Ra. with Bharati was in itself a clincher, as it revealed crucial aspects of the poet. Va. Ra. introduced himself to Bharati in English, which made the poet sad. Bharati found it both incongruous and slavish to be introduced to each other in a language that belonged to the colonial oppressors and not in their native tongue. For Va. Ra., it was a lesson learnt for life. From then on, he began to view English in almost the same light afforded to him by Bharati's perspective.

That also led Va. Ra. to develop a deep respect and love for Bharati that lasted all his life.

Bharati's attitude to English deserves to be studied in some detail. He had a good command over the English language, as evidenced by his writings in English. Yet, he could not see it wholly as a language without associating it with the British rule of India. In that he was quite unlike Rabindranath Tagore, who, according to renowned economist Amartya Sen, opposed the British rule but showed a favourable disposition towards the English language.[5] Tagore thought that English would influence Bengali literature through its poetry. Bharati was no less influenced by English poetry. He had called himself 'Shelleydas' (an acolyte of Shelley). His first published poem in 1904 was a sonnet, a well-known form of English poetry in fourteen lines that originated in Italy. His prose poems were the direct influence of his liking of the blank verse of Walt Whitman. He wanted the riches of the Tamil language to be known to others, by which he meant that Tamil works should be known through translations into other languages, including English. As a translator he appreciated English, and concluded that it taught him more of the nuances of Tamil in the process. He advised musicians to learn English and spread the glory of Carnatic music through it. But, despite them, the reasons for his professed hatred of the English language were many and deep rooted.

Even as a school-going student, Bharati had shown a dislike towards pursuing his studies in the English medium. His father, Chinnasamy Iyer, wanted him to be 'English educated' to qualify for a lucrative career as a lawyer. Owing to his poor financial status, he could not support Bharati's education. Bharati, being a subject of the *Ettayapuram Samasthan* (a Dominion or a princely state),[6] took the opportunity to request Ettayapuram Zamindar to provide him with money, but not for continuing his studies in the English medium as before. He wanted to pursue his studies in Tamil, and in that direction, he wrote a letter poem, the earliest of his extant writings, to the Ettayapuram Zamindar, fancying himself as the sole guardian of the Tamil language.

> 'Oh, Lord! My father who is here to make a living
> Forces me to learn an alien language. What shall I do?
> If I don't pursue to learn my sweet Tamil
> Then no one will
> Hence I dare to learn it
> But then, oh generous Lord, how can I ever learn without money?'

An important incident in his early life could have helped aggravate his feelings against the British government and consequently English, the language of the rulers. Bharati's father ran a factory called Ettayapuram Cotton Gin Factory Ltd in Ettayapuram. The British government, determined to crush all indigenous efforts to build a self-reliant economy, caused the factory's ruin. His father became bankrupt and died. Bharati was then sixteen years old. It had been pointed out that that experience had left him shattered, and the seeds of his deep hatred for the British were sown then.

Despite his unfavourable attitude towards English, Bharati wrote in English from time to time. He wrote letters to English papers whenever he wanted to express himself on important political matters. He translated into English the works of Tamil poets and his own poems to get the attention of the non-Tamil speaking world.[7] His richly allegorical satire, originally written in English, *Fox With the Golden Tail,* was widely appreciated when published, but it had occasioned Bharati to compare its success with the poor reception he got for his Tamil works. Nevertheless, he welcomed English words entering Tamil vocabulary as technical terms, and again that too only when suitable words for them were not to be found in Tamil and Sanskrit.[8]

But his outspoken dislike for English, had stood in his favour in more ways than one. Bharati's credo – 'As far as possible I will talk in Tamil. I will write in Tamil. I will think in Tamil.' – brought in a welcome attitude among Tamils. But it did not stop Tamil pundits, who were jealous of Bharati's astounding skills in poesy, from finding fault with him for not knowing Tamil grammar well. At the same time, they could not let out their jealousy for his knowledge of English. This triggers a comparison between Bharati and Tagore once again. Indo-Anglian writer Nirad. C. Chaudhuri observed that Tagore's proficiency in English was something his fellow Bengali writers could not stomach when his English translation of his own collection of poems *Gitanjali* won the Nobel Prize for Literature in 1913.[9] Bharati never won any worthy awards during his lifetime, but his familiarity with English did not give any occasion for Tamil pundits to develop jealousy towards him. Bharati, by always denigrating the use of English, showed everyone that he was not bathing in the glory of his English mastery, and that naturally took the wind out of their sails.

But there was another lesson, much more serious and important, that Va. Ra. learnt from Bharati, which made deep inroads in the way he looked at his own people. He saw Bharati not only teach, but also practise, his principles in his own life. So when others tried to picture Bharati as one who had been wise but not suited to the ways of the world, Va. Ra. let out his fury in defence of his mentor.

After Bharati's death, Rajaji (C. Rajagopalachari), who played a significant role in Indian politics both before and after Independence, summed up that Bharati became a staunch Vedanta adherent in his later years. Rajaji was not content with merely calling Bharati a Vedantist for his philosophical moorings, but went further to establish that even his patriotic songs originated from Vedanta. To Va. Ra. this was plain abuse of Bharati's reputation as a pragmatist, as one who was relentlessly in the pursuit of India's independence and the amelioration of the ills of society. He accused Rajaji of placing Bharati in a tiny Vedanta casket. Va. Ra. explained what Vedanta meant to Bharati.

"Bharati loathed the basic Maya concept of Vedanta. 'The wife stands like a golden statue. She melted in cries over our sorrows. She glowed with joy over our happiness. She brought up our children. Was she an illusion?' Bharati asked with anguish. To call Bharati a Vedantist is a big blunder. Besides, the contention of a few that the final growth of a person as a Vedantist is in consonance with the spirit of the land has led to perversities."

No doubt Bharati was a spiritual person. He was closely drawn to Vedanta. But Bharati was not a professional philosopher intending to develop and safeguard a system of thoughts. He rejoiced by singing the praises of the splendorous world before him. Sensory perceptions received unlimited attention in his appreciation of the world. Material world mattered to him no less. In his philosophical short novel *Gnanaratham* (Chariot of Wisdom), Bharati embarks on a dream journey to other worlds. The spiritual experience he derives chastens his vision. But he is absolutely against trading his earthly experience and beliefs for the permanent bliss the godly kingdoms might offer. Bharati was a man of the world, a man of *this* world. Precisely for this reason, no Vedantist is as fondly remembered and appreciated by people of various ideological hues as Bharati.

Va. Ra. once and for all defined Bharati unmistakably and succinctly, as follows: Bharati was not a sham Vedantist. He was a great poet. An artist without parallel. A true spirit who was born to rule and enjoy the world.

Truly, Bharati's eclecticism cannot be sourced to Vedanta philosophy.

There was however a slightly discordant note from Va. Ra. on a specific act of Bharati, when he converted a Dalit to a brahmin in Puducherry. Va. Ra. was witness to the anointing ceremony where R. Kanagalingam was converted to a brahmin by Bharati.[10] He wondered what orthodox madness drove Bharati, who had renounced the wearing of *poonool* (the sacred thread) himself, to do that to Kanagalingam.[11] Va. Ra. also followed Bharati on his iconoclastic path. Va. Ra.'s doubt was echoed later by many who questioned the rationale behind this act. Bharati opposed the sham orthodoxy at all levels. None had as severely ridiculed and condemned the servile brahmins who kowtowed to the British government for bureaucratic favours as Bharati during his life.

But he stoutly believed in the ideal of brahminhood. He sought to explain the brahmin as a selfless creature who worked for the welfare of others and who earned the caste title by his deeds and not automatically by birth. He continued the argument that if anyone purely by accidental virtue of his birth could assume a superior social status, then the concept of that practice should be decried forthwith and what better way lay before him than to demonstrate its elevated ideal by inducting one belonging to a caste outside it – and choosing especially

Kanagalingam, a Dalit to don an upper caste symbol? Bharati set out to question and expose a practice that he thought had derailed the ideal, reduced it to mumbo jumbo, and thereby inflicted harm to society. Bharati, by that single act, symbolically ripped off the assumption of the status of the upper caste. The influence obviously had come from the great Vaishnavite sage Ramanujar, who had performed the *poonool* ceremony (known as *Upanayanam*) not on a few, but on several, lower caste people, more than a thousand years ago. Bharati conducted the ceremony without publicity; Va. Ra. himself was on the scene by accident.

An important event in Bharati's life, which was a well settled affair for Va. Ra. and others, but that had become worrisome for his admirers later, was the letter Bharati wrote for release when he was in prison. Va. Ra. gives a detailed account of the circumstances under which it was obtained in the book. At that time he was not with Bharati, as Bharati had left Puducherry in 1914. But, Va. Ra. had given the reasons why Bharati wanted to leave Puducherry in the first place.

Bharati was of the opinion that the First World War would bring many benefits to India. In 1918, he came to know that his dream had been meaningless. After that, he did not like to live in Puducherry. He decided to return to British India. He wrote to A. Rangasamy Iyengar on that. Iyengar suggested that it was the ideal time for his return. As soon as Bharati crossed the boundary of the French government-occupied Puducherry, he was arrested by the British India police and held in the Cuddalore Sub Jail.

In fact he would have done worse if he had not exercised that option. He was weary both mentally and physically. He was not getting enough financial support from his friends. He was followed everywhere by the secret police. Puducherry life itself was a prison of sorts for him and his family. The First World War had brought Great Britain and France closer, and the possibility that he would be handed over from French territory to British India as a prisoner could not be overlooked. Weighed down by such factors, he wanted to enter India as a free man. Above all, the country occupied by the Britishers was his homeland, and naturally, he wanted to live there.

After his arrest, he was lodged in Cuddalore Sub Jail for twenty-four days. He had not left any account of his prison days. But, he wanted to get out of it at the earliest. Va. Ra. had written of the efforts made by A. Rangasamy Iyengar, then the editor of *Swadesamitran*, who prepared a letter on Bharati's behalf. It was addressed to Lord Pentland, Governor, Fort St. George. It mentioned, among other things, that henceforth he would renounce politics and pursue the life of a peaceful citizen in British India, and added that 'the conditions in prison were altogether disagreeable to a man of my birth and status, and full of dangerous possibilities to my health', and hence he sought release. Whether Bharati fully approved the draft and then signed it, or he signed it out of desperation to end his time in prison, which could have been extended to any length, no one would ever know. The tenor and wording of the letter clearly establish that Bharati did not have a hand in it, for it is quite unlike anything he had written all his life. But, to his readers, who were reared by his exhortations to maintain fearlessness even if the heavens were to fall on their heads, the text of the letter would be truly disconcerting, just as the studied silence maintained by him over the arrest of M. Srinivasan Iyengar, the scapegoat of an editor of *India*. It was not known if Va. Ra. had the occasion to peruse the copy of the letter himself. The letter was made public much later.[12]

Va. Ra.'s admiration for Bharati grew more and more as time went on. In 1935, Va. Ra., in an article, extolled Bharati as a great poet without any parallel. The trouble arose not because Bharati was favourably compared to great poets, but because others, in comparison to him, were unfavourably belittled. This was taken for a debate by the well-known Tamil novelist Kalki. Many jumped into the fray, arguing for and against, while Va. Ra. held court. Tamil writers, Chitti and Ku. Pa. Rajagopalan, wrote in defence of Va. Ra.'s arguments favouring Bharati, and their articles were published in 1937 as a book titled *Kannan En Kavi*. Later the debate was settled, and Bharati was accepted as one who took his poetry to epic proportions. He was hailed as the successor of Kamban, who wrote the finest Tamil epic *Ramayanam*.

Tamil poets of yore were discussed, debated and feted in royal courts, but only Bharati was argued for and against in a government assembly under foreign rule. Bharati was a Congress Party man, and he sang his songs on its political platforms. After his death, his songs were banned in Burma (now Myanmar) and based on that, the ban was imposed in India also. The Congress leader and Parliamentarian S. Sathiyamurthy, mustering all his eloquence, argued against the ban in the Madras Legislative Assembly, asserting that if Bharati had been born in England he would have been its poet laureate.[13]

Since Va. Ra. had too well established Bharati

aesthetically, others began to see his power as a thinker and social reformer on a broader level. He was chiefly approached from political angles.

Because of his rejection of caste, Bharati was praised by leaders of the Dravidian movement, though he was not considered an insider. At every available opportunity, in prose and poems, and also in his missives to newspapers and journals, Bharati lashed out at the caste system with brave and unequivocal candour. When a debate raged over the merits of caste hierarchy, he reacted sharply with his letter to the editor of *New India*. Now that India is awakening to a New Age, it will be well for my Brahmana countrymen if they voluntarily relinquish all their old pretensions together with the silly and anti-national customs based on such pretensions, and lead the way for the establishment of liberty, equality, and fraternity among Indians.[14]

He was often quoted by Dravidian leaders in support of their attacks on the Brahminical ideology and its practices. Dravida Munnetra Kazhagam (DMK) founder and former chief minister of Tamil Nadu, C. N. Annadurai patronisingly noted that if Bharati had been offered a choice to choose between Aryan and Dravidian cultures, he would have doubtlessly chosen the latter; only such an opportunity did not present itself while he was alive.[15] His successor and five-time chief minister of the DMK regime, M. Karunanidhi, borrowed the words from Bharati's poem as the title for his autobiography *Nenjukku Needhi*. Bharatidasan, the Dravidian poet laureate, with unstinted admiration and respect, adored Bharati all his life and that was an exception among Dravidians.

The Marxists, unlike those owing allegiance to Dravidian ideologies, were not hesitant to embrace him as the modern Tamil poet closest to their philosophy due to several strong reasons. It was Bharati who coined the Tamil word 'Puratchi' (Revolution), a word with ideological underpinnings associated with the political left. Also, Bharati was the only major Asian poet who wrote a poem heralding the Bolshevik Revolution just fourteen days after it had taken place. He was not a poet closely associated with the Socialist revolution in Russia, yet he had absorbed its historical importance in all its plenitude,[16] as one that ushered in a new era based on socialism and stamped out a cruel monarchy. Sri Lankan Tamil academic K. Kailasapathy observed that Bharati intuitively understood Dialectical Materialism because of his ability to judge the conflict between the old and the new. He further stated that Bharati was the forerunner among his contemporaries, who could think of a new social order where the working class would be the shaping force of history, aligning with the outcome of the socialist revolution.[17]

Bharati had sung about the importance of the working class and the indigenous production of materials ranging from nails to warships for winning India's freedom. He wanted fixed working hours for the workers. He welcomed the formation of trade unions and went on to exhort them to extend their activities by conducting classes, even organizing night schools for their cadres; for without education, workers would not be fully benefitted in their trade. His attack on upper castes also stemmed from the realization that they exploited the labour of the working class. He dedicated his story *Aaril Oru Pangu* (One Sixth) to farmers, who formed one sixth of the population.

P. Jeevanandham, a leader of the Communist Party of India, was foremost among those who appreciated Bharati wholeheartedly. He used his political platforms to sing the praise of Bharati. As the Tamil writer Pe. Su. Mani had mentioned, Jeevanandham was chiefly responsible for developing the Marxist perception of Bharati. He was also the first public figure to demand the nationalization of Bharati's works. Bharati's works were taken to Soviet Russia and studied with due attention because of the Marxists. The Marxists' share in the pie of his fame was significant. From Va. Ra.'s account, we learn that Bharati was never in the mood to hurt the pride of the working class. When the needle of suspicion for the theft of a manuscript in Bharati's household pointed towards a domestic help, Bharati looked aside and defended him because he was 'one of us'.

Only Va. Ra. was witness to Bharati's birth pangs while conceiving a poem and his ecstasy on its delivery. I resist the strong impulse to quote from the book even a sentence of it since I do not want the readers to get deprived of the thrill of wholly experiencing it themselves.

On many occasions, Va. Ra. found Bharati suffering without means. He was often paid inadequately and, during hard times, he also suffered without income due to his position as a fugitive. On such occasions, Bharati himself had lamented that if he were to be worrying about 'salt and rice', then how could he write poems peacefully. At the same time, Bharati treated the circumstances of his poverty lightly and humorously, and conducted himself majestically.

But he is being projected as one who was eternally poor. Such a warped image of him helps the Tamil public that is too ready to blame the times of Bharati to gain its own moral superiority for neglecting him. It has alongside aided in carving out an image of the poet as selfless and oblivious to the needs of himself and his family. It has also shamelessly cultivated a perception that for a writer to be genuine he should have chosen poverty, and aspiring for riches would nip off the creative buds. Va. Ra. records one such attitude in the book. Once, Bharati wrote a letter to a friend asking for a small sum of money. His friend saw him in the evening and gave a fantastic explanation for not sending the money. Financial help would have made Bharati complacent and robbed him of his poetic sharpness, were the explanations offered by him.

"Bharati, when he heard the explanation, became terribly angry. 'Stop your bragging. Is poverty not enough for an intellectual? Should he also be ridiculed for it? You cannot be reformed. This country needs a revolutionary philosophy to crush it altogether.' Bharati blasted him and left the place. Those who dared to insult the indigence of the poets are scum who would never understand the true nature of emotions," wrote Va. Ra.

It should be remembered that Bharati lived all his life as a journalist, and his income would have enabled him to put food on the table. It was on a monthly salary that he joined *Swadesamitran*. As the unofficial editor of *India*, he was paid a monthly salary of fifty rupees, which was a decent sum during the years 1906–08.[18] Even when he was in Puducherry, he received a monthly allowance of thirty rupees from *Swadesamitran*, as Va. Ra. has attested. He has also pointed out that the sum of thirty rupees, during the period Bharati was in Puducherry (between 1908–18), was equivalent to one hundred rupees in the 1940s.[19] Va. Ra. bore witness to an occasion in Puducherry when Bharati received a substantial sum of one thousand rupees from Durban. When he relocated to Chennai, after his release from prison, his monthly salary as an assistant editor at *Swadesamitran* was fifty rupees. His legendary generosity while neglecting domestic needs often landed him in deep financial trouble and led to frequent domestic squabbles.[20] Va. Ra. decried the attitude of lauding poverty and firmly believed that it was not in the Indian ethos.

Our platform speakers wrongly say that the base of our civilization is destitution. In other words, simplicity and despair. And such civilization is unequalled in the world. When the white man brought the civilization of wealth and comfortable living to our country, our ancient simplicity and despair left us without any trace. That shows our people did not accept despair wholeheartedly, since it was imposed on them for generations. Was it not made clear that when the opportunity came, our people were ready to shun it?

Another aspect which he found lacking in the Tamil people was the inability to identify talent that lay before them. He launched blistering attacks on his contemporaries, including Rajaji and S. Sathiyamurthy, for recognizing Bharati's greatness only belatedly.[21] Many, even today, talk glowingly of ancient works but with no knowledge of contemporary literature.

Va. Ra.'s missionary zeal to establish Bharati as a great poet is at the base of all that had taken place subsequently. Va. Ra. not only wrote on Bharati, but he also shared his ideals. Whenever Bharati is remembered among his contemporaries, Va. Ra. is also remembered together with Bharati, like Samuel Johnson and his biographer James Boswell. Such instances are rare in the annals of the literary history of the world.

Va. Ra.'s biography, besides focusing on Bharati, is a veritable gallery of portraits of the people associated with him. All those who were his friends, acquaintances, disciples and common folks in contact with him and the police who shadowed him are presented with their characteristics. More than the well-known people who associated with him on important matters, the relatively unknown people come out as strikingly human and noteworthy. Ammakannu is one such person. Va. Ra.'s portrait of her is the most moving piece in the book. A household maid, old and poor, she looked after Bharati without expecting anything in return from him during his trying times. Sundaresa Iyer, Muthialpet Krishnasamy Chettiar, Ponnu Murugesan Pillai, Murugesan, Raja Bahadur and his mother are some among many of the unforgettable people who flit through the pages of the book. There is also a tender account of a boy with an unsound mind brought back to normalcy by Bharati.

There is a description of a crucial event, in the biography that had supposedly led to Bharati's death. Bharati used to feed the elephant at the Triplicane Parthasarathy Temple every day, according to Va. Ra., with brotherly affection. One day it behaved differently, and pushed him onto the ground. His friend Kuvalai Kannan rescued him immediately. Va. Ra. said that the internal injuries caused by the elephant resulted in his death three months later. He also surmised that the contrary attitude of the elephant could have been viewed by Bharati, unbeknownst to others, as betrayal of his faith in the animal.

What Bharati might have felt of his relationship with the elephant after the accident is anyone's guess. Whether he died of the injuries inflicted on him by the elephant attack, and if his death took place three months thereafter or not, are matters, however, not easily settled. Even sources close to him had given varying accounts. But there is strong evidence that Bharati was deeply depressed after his release from prison. He was not happy with his own attitude in the letter given for early release. His health steadily deteriorated in his final years and above all, he refused to take medicine. Those were certainly the factors that should have contributed to his death. Even if one were to assume that the pachyderm's sudden attack took place in the middle of 1921, it could not have been responsible for his death since he recovered shortly from the shock and the minor injuries caused by his fall, and resumed his duties in *Swadesamitran* office.[22]

Subramania Bharati was born to Chinnasamy Subramania Iyer and Lakshmi Ammal on 11 December 1882 in Ettayapuram and died on 12 September 1921 in Chennai. He lived less than thirty-nine years. Within that short and active life, he left deep imprints on everything he touched. As his wife Chellammal had endearingly noted, Bharati completed his duties hurriedly in life, and when the time approached he died hurriedly too, as though he was completing another duty.

In Va. Ra.'s biography, Bharati emerges as a great poet who wrote for the masses and who lived with the masses, an inclusive nationalist in mainstream politics, a champion of women's freedom and social causes, a reformer who assailed casteism, an innovative journalist who was sensitive to the vibrant happenings of the world, and an extraordinary human being who literally gave the shirt he was wearing to anyone who was unable to have one.

2

Va. Ra. (full name V. Ramaswamy Iyengar), born on 17 September 1889 to Varadaraja Iyengar and Ponnammal in Thingalur village of Thanjavur District, was the eldest of seven siblings. He had his primary school education in a 'Thinnai Pallikudam' of those days, so named because the elementary school was conducted on the *pyol* (a raised platform outside a house/building on which people can sit or lie down) of a building, in his native village. He went to high school in Tiruvaiyaru and passed the matriculation exams. He could not pass in his F.A. (Faculty of Arts) exams. But he wanted to continue his higher studies and hence he went to Calcutta to join the college founded by Surendranath Bannerjee, the educationist and freedom fighter. He could not get admission there, and returned to Tamil Nadu.

He went on to Puducherry as an envoy of Kodiyalam V. Rangasamy Iyengar, who was his patron for his education, to meet Aurobindo Ghose before in June 1911. There he met Subramania Bharati. He was then twenty-one years old, which was not exactly an impressionable age. But from his first meeting onwards, he was captivated by the rigorous intellectual charm of Bharati. He became a staunch devotee of Bharati for the rest of his life. Bharati introduced him to Aurobindo as the patriot from Tamil Nadu. Then one of the patriots assembled there jibed him:

"'Did not he know an application to the government had to be made before entering Puducherry?' and laughed, and he was followed by others except Bharati."

Va. Ra. was taken for a coward as he entered incognito. But in their case, the government knew of their arrival because of their reputation as patriotic bravehearts.

Va. Ra. has recorded what happened after: "I smiled sheepishly! But Bharati betrayed no emotion. He came down with a blast. 'Among slaves do the Bengalis score higher over Tamils?' That gave me the guts to raise my head." Va. Ra. wrote that only after meeting Bharati did he understand what patriotism really meant.

During his stay there, for thirty-one months, he was in constant contact with both Bharati and Aurobindo. The learning of Bengali, through Aurobindo's contact, and the desire to write in Tamil, under the influence of Bharati, who wanted the riches of other languages to be brought into Tamil, resulted in him the desire to translate Bankim Chandra Chatterjee's Bengali short novel *Jugalanguriya* into Tamil as *Jodi Mothiram* (The Two rings).[23] It is said that Bharati caught him in the act of translating the novella, and conveyed his appreciation of the work in the presence of Aurobindo. Typical of Bharati, after lavishing his praise on the translation, he went on to the extent of saying that henceforth he would concentrate on poetry alone, since Tamil prose would be taken care of by Va. Ra. As time went on, Va. Ra. grew closer to Bharati and like Bharati, he too distanced himself from Aurobindo, the reason for which is given in the book. It was ironic that the man who went to meet Aurobindo ended up as a devotee of Bharati and wrote his biography. Va. Ra.'s biography, though short on complete details, is the most spirited account of the poet's life. It is to be borne in mind that he himself nurtured the thought of writing a full-scale biography of Bharati at a later date.

Va. Ra. left Puducherry on 21 January 1914. His recording of meeting Bharati in 1919 was memorable for more than one reason. It was then that he witnessed the meeting of Bharati and Gandhi, and the historic details associated with it were given to posterity only by him. It is surprising that Bharati had not written about Va. Ra. in public. He had only mentioned him in a letter he wrote to his brother, C. Viswanatha Iyer, in connection with the publication of a few of his works.[24] The reason could be that while he was with Bharati, Va. Ra. was seen as a polite disciple and had not tried to impress him in any manner other than as a budding translator. It is not known whether Bharati had read Va. Ra.'s maiden novel *Sundari* published in 1917. But Va. Ra. continued to write about Bharati reverentially, and carried forward his ideals by practising them in his life. Apart from his indefatigable defence of Bharati as a great poet, he was also one of those instrumental in the nationalisation of his works.

Va. Ra. entered politics early in life. In his college days he was reprimanded by the College Principal for chanting Vande Mataram. He joined the Congress party and for his participation in the Salt Satyagraha in 1930, he was imprisoned in Alipore Jail for six months.

Along with his literary friends, he founded *Manikodi* magazine in 1933, which exerted a great influence on Tamil writing. But Va. Ra. didn't continue in it for long. He went to Sri Lanka and joined *Virakesari* in 1935 as an assistant editor. In Sri Lanka too he spoke on Bharati in various meetings. In 1936 he married Bhuvaneswari, a widow – not a common practice in those times. He returned to Chennai in 1937, and associated with All India Radio broadcasts. In September 1948, he participated in the First Bharati Memorial celebrated in Ettayapuram. There, he was presented with a purse and with that, he bought a house in Chennai. He never enjoyed good health in all his life, and died on 23 August 1951 at the age of sixty-two. He expressed his wish to be cremated without any religious rites; and that was what he had done with his own three-month-old child when she died.

The Tamil Nadu Government granted his widow a monthly pension in 1990.

Va. Ra., besides his career as a journalist, was a writer of short stories, novels, and essays. At a time when popular writing was meant to titillate the readers, he remained a purposeful writer. For him, writing was meant to serve social purposes. He contended that art and morality were two sides of the same coin. When what he saw as the strength of India was slandered, he resorted to polemics. In that vein, he wrote a book-length rebuttal *Maya Mayo Allathu Mayovukku Savukkadi* (Mayo's Illusion or Whiplash to Mayo) to Katherine Mayo's book *Mother India,* which asserted that Indians were incapable of self-rule. But Va. Ra. was not the one who supported the past for its own sake. He never yearned to go back to earlier times, and always wanted to march ahead in the direction guided by reason and scientific knowledge. He wrote in easily intelligible Tamil that was closer to speech. He did not favour *Thaniththamizh* or 'Pure Tamil', a linguistic movement that insisted strictly on the use of words of Tamil origin.

Va. Ra. wrote four novels spanning four decades. In three of them, he deals with child marriage and child widowhood in the Brahminical households which act as a prism that reflects the regressive morals affecting the country as a whole. *Sundari,* his first novel, was written in 1917. Its publication was well-received by the public despite its content, that was too bold for its time. It prompted C. N. Annadurai to admiringly call

Va. Ra. as *Agraharathu Athisaya Piravi*,[25] 'The wonder being of Agraharam' (Agraharam is the community settlement of brahmins). *Sundari* and *Vijayam* (1944), the eponymous heroines of his novels, are child widows. So is Nagammal in *Chinna Sambu* (1942). Both Sundari and Nagammal, after undergoing their travails, find life support through remarriage. Of the three, Vijayam is the unluckiest as she does not enter remarriage but she emerges as the most audacious female voice against child widowhood among Va. Ra.'s heroines.

Va. Ra. brilliantly brings out the female sexuality to the fore through Vijayam and another old woman Janu, in *Vijayam*. There is an unforgettable scene in the novel where Janu, who was also widowed as a child and is now in her sixties, shares with Vijayam and Vijayam's grandmother a memory of a sexual relationship she had with a pundit many years ago. It is revealed in privacy, and both the listeners show profound sympathy to Janu. It shows that despite around-the-clock vigil by the custodians of patriarchy, there was still a private world which was all women. In T. Janakiraman's *Amma Vanthal* (1966), Krithika's *Vasaveswaram* (1966), and Ashokamitran's *Manasarovar* (1989), the arousal of the female sexuality has found its expression in varying degrees. But in *Vijayam*, earlier than all of these, it is unveiled through frank discussions conducted by women themselves.

In 1945, Va. Ra. also wrote a utopian novel *Kothai Theevu* (Island of Women), in which the rulers are all women. It was for the first time that Va. Ra. stepped out of his committed theme of widow remarriage, and visualized an imaginary republic to find solutions to the gnawing problems of society. But Va. Ra. was clearly out of his element here. He ends up conjuring a world that is less than ideal. *Kothai Theevu* is all about a regimented colony where its subjects are moulded into automatons.

As a fiction writer, Va. Ra.'s talents are second to none who use fiction as an art form. He creates a vast array of characters and develops situations that take the narrative swiftly forward. His fiction writings also adequately present the social milieu of the times. Yet, by an apparent design, Va. Ra. wields his creative talents to engage the reader frontally without waxing into subtleties. He raises an alarm and urges them to act against injustice meted out to people in the name of protection of Hindu orthodoxy, concerning chiefly, female chastity and caste hierarchy. There are no sentimental lacings in his portrayal of the characters in distress. He speaks for their rights and strikes at the conscience of the reader to take responsibility for the prevailing state of affairs. Bharati's influence on him can be seen throughout. Quotes from Bharati are everywhere in his works. But as a fiction writer, Bharati did not provoke the reader as much as Va. Ra. did in his novels. As storytellers, Bharati was a litterateur as provocateur, while Va. Ra. was a provocateur as litterateur.

His short stories in the collection titled *Katrathu Kutrama* (Is Knowledge a Crime?) are narrated in a lighter and often melodramatic vein. Love for Tamil, heroic valour, romantic love unto death, caste barriers that prove fatal in love relationship, aspiring for Gandhian idealism, and the double standards of a man who displays a reforming spirit, are the subjects of the stories. As compared to his novels, he exhibits a certain sensitivity to the form of the short story, though that would not be what one would expect of a writer belonging to the *Manikodi* literary tradition, known for its extraordinary achievements in that genre.

Of significant importance was his series of essays, admittedly written under the influence of the English essayist A. G. Gardiner, under the rubric *Nadai Chitram* (Pen Portraits), where Va. Ra. portrayed people from every walk of life. He had picked many who belonged to the lower rungs of society. Simple folks such as the cart driver, the street hawker, the tribal woman who was a tattoo artist and a fortune-teller, the watchman, the do-gooder orphan, the washerman and the housemaid all figured in them, along with others who belonged to higher stations in society. He did not directly identify any living person. It is proper to say that they were closely modelled on the people he saw in daily life. These journalistic sallies were immediately appreciated, and influenced a host of writers. Chitti wrote that the writers of *Manikodi* magazine tried to imitate them. Pudumaipithan's *Tirukural Kumaresa Pillai* followed in that vein.[26] Later on, their influence could be seen notably in Kalki's *Yaar Intha Manithargal*? (Who Are They?) Jayakanthan's encounter with people in a mental asylum and in everyday life in *Avargal Ulle Irukirargal* (They Remain Inside) and *Silar Veliye Irukirargal* (Some People Remain Outside), respectively, also betrayed Va. Ra.'s influence.

Va. Ra.'s biographical portraits were collected in *Thamizh Periyorgal* (Tamil Savants). In them, due to his broad vision of life, he brought in people from the fields of cinema and theatre, realizing the important positions they held in public life, including S. S. Vasan, K. B. Sundarambal, and N. S. Krishnan, and placed them at par with well-known and well-respected people: E. V. R. Periyar, C. Rajagopalachari, Thiru. Vi. Kalayanasundara Mudaliar, Dr P. Varadarajalu Naidu, and Dr T. S. S. Rajan, among others. Not many during those times took people from the 'entertainment world' as seriously as Va. Ra. did. He also argued the case for a not too well-known freedom fighter, George Joseph, to be included among them.

Another notable work of Va. Ra. was the imaginary encounters held among various literary and historical personages from the past. Titled *Suvarkathil Sambashanai* (Conversation in Heaven), every piece in it featured conversations between two people with similar associations, but belonging to different time periods. In some of them, explanations were demanded from a modernist point of view, for the 'lapses' committed by the predecessors. It was as if Va. Ra. was rewriting the past according to his predilections. They were modelled on Walter Savage Landor's 'Imaginary Conversations'.

Va. Ra. liked plays and had written a one-act play on Ramanujar. He also wrote the dialogue for the film *Ramanujar* in 1938. He favoured *Tamil Isai* and paid rich tributes to stage singer S. G. Kittappa for taking it to the masses. His translations included Jawaharlal

Nehru's autobiography. He was a very well-read man. His English article, 'What is Poetry', written when he was in Alipore Jail, is proof of his wide scholarship, as are several other pieces by him. Perhaps the work which he dearly wanted to do, but did not, was the publication of Bharati's works.[27]

In all his writings, Va. Ra. lampooned and harshly criticized the meaningless religious rituals and other worldly practices of his countrymen. He was admired for his steadfast ideals, and the unsympathetic attitude shown to him by the orthodox was understandable. He preferred to dine with everyone at a time when commensal dining was frowned upon. It was said, that in his younger days, when the people in the Agraharam in his native village objected to carrying the dead body of a Dalit through their streets, Va. Ra. took a bold stand against them and facilitated the funeral procession to pass through.[28] His attitude in public and private was that of a rebel. His greatest inspiration in life was Subramania Bharati, and his most enduring portrait was *Mahakavi Bharatiyar*.

Amshan Kumar

Translator's Note

ELSEWHERE IN THE BOOK, VA. RA. HAS PRONOUNCED rigorous rules for translation. As the translator, I have not done a literal translation but tried to be as close to the spirit of the text as possible. It has many allusions to names, places, and events. Va. Ra. himself has written about a good many of them in the book adequately. The book abounds with the mention of many well-known people, and they naturally do not need any additional description. I have provided brief notes for a select few to place them in their context.

Despite his claim that he approached knowledgeable sources to avoid factual errors in narrating Bharati's life, it is obvious from the flow of the text that Va. Ra. has written much of the biography without preparatory notes, and hence certain inaccuracies with regard to their time references have crept in. Corrective details for them are given in the footnotes and in the notes at the end.

The author has not used italics in his work. In the translation, they are used for titles of works by Bharati, and for certain words for which meanings and additional information are given in parentheses. Other than these, the parentheses are from the original text. The footnotes are mine.

Va. Ra. mentions Bharati as 'Bharatiyar' throughout the book and also elsewhere in his writings. The name 'Bharati', when conjoined with the 'ar' suffix, is Bharatiyar. The Tamil 'ar' suffix is added to the name Bharati out of respect, and in that Va. Ra. follows the tradition of other Tamils when they mention the names of people they revere and respect. Readers will find in the book the virulent exception Bharati and his friends took when a Tamil lawyer mentioned Tilak as such, and not as 'Thilagar' as he was respectfully called, using Tamil spelling and the 'ar' suffix. In the translation Bharatiyar is Bharati, as he is known originally without the suffix.

Meanings of words that are not of English origin and must be understood immediately are given in the text itself and not in the glossary, traditionally found at the end of the book.

I express my sincere thanks to Anubha Roy and T. Ramakrishnan for their valuable suggestions.

Finally, I gratefully acknowledge the wholehearted support given by N. Muruganandam for this effort.

A. K.

Preface

THE BIOGRAPHICAL ACCOUNT THAT I HAVE WRITTEN on Bharati is incomplete. Whether matters are related to politics or literature or social problems – in everything our society is under the rule of tyranny. Therefore our people suffer without freedom of expression.

If we talk about politics, the Indian Minister Amery gets angry.[1] He thinks India is his private property.

If we talk about literature, the Pure Tamil pundits curse people like me as sinners born to ruin Tamil. In these days of democracy, the notion of Pure Tamil pundits that Tamil is their own property, is peculiar.

If we talk about social problems, conservatives and grandmas become wrathful. Just as the slum dwellers told Nandan that his habits did not conform to their customs, these people talk nonsensically that such things are against our tradition.[2]

Therefore those who desire freedom on these three fronts encounter many struggles. When freedom is denied, speech and writing cannot bring forth complete truth and sublimeness. I do not want to substitute a crude piece in the place of a magnificent work. Hence I have to leave many things unsaid.

Many more matters have to be told in an upright manner. But even God cannot wait for the waves to subside for him to take a bath. It is not expedient to defer writing about Bharati until India gets Independence.

Canards on Bharati are in circulation. Those who saw him with dread and those who dreaded to see him are now falsely spreading stories of the close contact they had had with him. I do not know what to say of the people who beat their chests feigning grief overly when death occurs in the abode of the rich.

I have condensed the book with the hope that I can write about Bharati in elaborate detail in a few years' time.

Nungambakkam **Va. Ra.**

1-9-1944

1

"WHAT IMPUDENCE! CAN'T YOU SEE IT?" EXCLAIMED MY friend Kesavan.[1]

I was clueless, like anyone would be, when something like this came without a prelude.

Kesavan went on with a pitched fervour. "Do you remember the poem lamenting the demise of Pillai Pandian, Villiputhuraar, and Ottakoothar, that had given room for upstarts to indulge in poetry?[2] In the wake of Bharati's death, similarly several namesakes have spawned in a shameless manner."

"Let them do as they might in good number, but is not their borrowing his name in itself an acceptance of Bharati's greatness?" I said. Would a doting wife ever bear to listen if some other woman mentioned her husband's name coquettishly? Kesavan was in a similar position when Bharati's name was adopted by lesser poets.

"Do you remember or should I remind you?" asked my friend.

"Don't I know the sayings in Tamil that a single branding of a bull by a flaming iron rod and a word of censure to a woman will suffice to set them in order? Likewise I am alert to the promise I have made."

"Well then. Narrate in detail since you first met Bharati."

I give him credit for providing the stimulus to unfold my account of Bharati.

"Delay no further. Start your narration," he enjoined me.

"Here it goes, my pal. If anyone by chance had the occasion to skim through the dailies published in March and April 1910, they would have come across amusing headlines like, 'Where did he go? How did he go there? To Geneva City in Switzerland?'"

"Did they refer to Bharati?"

"You are in for disappointment. They were not about Bharati but about Babu Aurobindo Ghose. It finally transpired that he had secretly reached Puducherry."

Kodiyalam V. Rangasamy Iyengar, who passed away recently, was an impeccable patriot. Truly a gentle spirit. He was devoted to Aurobindo. He asked me 'Is the information true that Aurobindo has reached Puducherry?'

'I can neither hazard a guess nor divine a prediction,' I replied. 'In that case, I curse you to go to Puducherry.'

'A rishi issues a curse on the strength of his penance. But when you curse, it should be backed by money.'

'Here, you have the money,' he said. I set out for Puducherry.

A few words before I embark on my journey.

I was not aware that Subramania Bharati was on the staff of the daily newspaper 'Swadesamitran' in 1910. But I knew he was working for the weekly magazine 'India'. While Bharati was in Chennai, he had two friends who were much older than him. Their admiration for him was not easy to describe. You might be startled if I were to mention their names.

One was the late V. Krishnasamy Iyer who served as a High Court Judge and also as a member of the Administrative office of the Governor. Another was A. Krishnasamy Iyer who retired as Deputy Police Commissioner. Those two Krishnasamy Iyers were inseparable friends. I came to know later that, at their insistence, Bharati had left for Puducherry.

I cannot but mention one immeasurable contribution made by V. Krishnasamy Iyer. During the times when the Tamils were too afraid of the tyranny of the British

Government, it was he who dared to publish Bharati's nationalist poems in two volumes.

I was one of those who were entranced by reading them. This happened prior to 1910.

I was doubly happy of the curse imposed on me by my friend Rangasamy Iyengar. In those times, the police would watch those entering Puducherry, French India's capital, having suspicious eye movements. Our grandmothers used to say 'It is dangerous to have a stiff neck.' I never had a stiff neck that would have made me look sideways to arouse suspicion. But I knew that sand could scorch more than the blazing sun. Iyengar was concerned about my safe journey without police intervention.

What should I say about myself? In my ecstatic state I was not too sure if I existed on planet Earth.

The train arrived at Puducherry at about 5.30 in the morning. I was not in the least worried if anyone ever cast his sight on me. It was no idle imagination that I felt like a beetle whirring above in the sky besotted with a drink of nectar. Everyone must have had a similar experience at least once in their lifetime.

I was unused to travelling by any mode of transport. It was believed that to ensure travel by foot, legs had been created. Well. You might laugh, treating it as a philosophy born of penury. Go ahead. Laughter speeds up digestion.

I had not previously seen the Puducherry pushcart. It suddenly occurred that to reach a significant place, I should also maintain style besides observing decorum. So I hailed a pushcart. But only the driver appeared, and not his vehicle.

'Do you know where Bharati lives?' I asked him.

'The man from *Pattanam* (Madras, now Chennai) who sings and sports a moustache? I know his house very well,' he responded.

I was familiar with his description of Bharati save the mention of his moustache. I had not seen him in the first place.

He pulled his cart in front of a house located at the far end of Eswaran Dharmaraja Koil Street. Some kind of mysterious fear suddenly replaced the joy I had been feeling until then. My heart raced fast. To camouflage my trepidation I overpaid the driver and dismissed him. Placing my left arm on my chest, I climbed up the stairs. I had no heavy luggage. All I carried was my own weight, clothes, and a few rupees. I have to admit that my eyes also carried slightly the additional burden of sleeplessness from the whole night.

'Sir,' I called. I repeated it again and yet again for the

third time. A young man with a strong, muscular build appeared.

He bluntly asked, 'Who?'

'Who? I am myself.'

He looked me up and down. I did the same to him. 'Who do you want?'

'Subramania Bharati.'

'Then come on.'

We reached the upper storey of the house. I caught sight of a man 'who sports a moustache'. I do not remember if he was clad in a shirt and *angavastram* (a long towel of high quality material worn stylishly around the neck by men). I prostrated myself before him. He lunged forward like a tiger and lifted me up.

'There is no need for prostration. Tell me who you are? Why have you come?' he asked.

I stood silently before him for some time.

'Well. Have you brushed your teeth? We can talk after breakfast. Balu, give him tooth powder and water.'

Balu was the name of the young man who had accosted me on the steps.[3]

While I was brushing my teeth, I saw an old man appear. 'Come on in, *Vilakkennai* Chettiar,' (a nickname for Sabapathy Chettiar) welcomed Bharati. How do I express the bodily contortions of Chettiar, despite the warm welcome accorded him? Do you know who Chettiar was? He was the landlord of Bharati's house. He would shudder to ask for even the house rent that was his due. He was fondly addressed by Bharati with the prefix *Vilakkennai* (castor oil) a nickname.

'Oh, Chettiar, what is the hurry for house rent? Being a Hindu, you are destined to be born several times to enjoy high positions. In another ten years India will get *Swaraj* (self-rule). I will issue a cheque to the state treasury. You can accept it now.' Having said that, he broke into a peal of laughter that sounded like incessant rapping on bronze. It was a laughter that poked fun at penury.

I curiously awaited Chettiar's reaction. He murmured. 'Great soul! Who said your cheque would not be valid? You can give that without further thought. I will accept it.'

'Chettiar! You will live for a hundred years. No sooner I get money, than I send it to you. Now you may go.' Chettiar disappeared after making a bow.

We ate something. I slowly opened up about the purpose of my visit.

'How do you know that Aurobindo Babu is here? I don't know that myself. So be it. Are you fond of Tamil songs?' he asked. I simply smiled.

'As a penalty for your smile you should listen to a song.'

"Do you think I had objection to the penalty he imposed on me, Kesav?"

"I can only be jealous of your good fortune," said Kesavan, who had never seen Bharati in person.

2

"Kesav! I was somewhat inaccurate in my narration. When Bharati lifted me up from his feet, he enquired about me.

I could have answered him in Tamil. But I poured forth in English as one who had learnt it with pride. Bharati shouted. 'Balu, this man equals you in English knowledge. You can talk to him. I have no business to do with him.' It was then that I understood his mental agony.

"'For how long should Tamils choose to talk in English among themselves?' He asked me in a saddened voice. I was overcome with emotion. I could not speak.

"He sang a song known to us as *Maravan Pattu* (Song of Maravan). His voice and the song enraptured me. I was beside myself with joy. I was transported to another realm altogether. I understood what the yogic condition truly meant. I came to my senses slowly.

Bharati caught me in my condition of bliss. We began to talk of our country's liberation.

"'Before attaining liberation for the country, we should get liberation for our nerves, our tongue, our poetry, our language,' he went on and on in this vein. I now understand that it was not meant as a florid declamation. For the first time in my life, the meaning of the word 'liberation' resonated with the idea of a nation through Bharati. That 'Tamil has glory to it and Tamilians have a pride of place' I understood firmly only after seeing Bharati. It is no mean imagination that it was only my acquaintance with Bharati that brought me the limitless joy of wisdom. Until then I was only chanting Vande Mataram with childish gusto.

"I experienced 'the honeyed voice of Tamil' coming directly from him.* I could not divine where I existed. That Tamil had a spirit, form, strength, grace, and distinctness that I understood only on that day.

"I expected that, like any other person, Bharati would ask me, 'How is the song?' I was afraid of saying merely, 'The song is good.'

Bharati understood my state of mind well. He sang a few more songs. I could not believe the good fortune I had.

---

* A reference to the poem 'Tamil' by Bharati, extolling the beauty of the Tamil language.

"Like the flooding of the ocean, the songs gushed forth rapidly. I was in a trance. Bharati stopped singing. Then we bathed and dined. At around four in the afternoon, Bharati called me, 'Let us go out.' We entered a house.

"'Bharati, please come in,' a man invited us in a sweet voice. He was Mandayam Srinivasachariar.

"'This friend wants to see that hardy man,' said Bharati to him. The man he referred to was none other than Aurobindo Ghose, I learnt. Despite the fact that they were in the throes of seeking political asylum in Puducherry, sarcasm and humour had not taken leave of the patriots.

'We will go and ask him. Then let fate take its own course,' said Srinivasachariar.

It dawned on me, from their speech, that Aurobindo was a man often given to aggressive moods. 'If it is bothersome then I don't want to meet him,' I said.

"'You should have thought of that earlier and saved the expenses of your trip to Puducherry,' said Bharati with a smile. I was in a fit of uneasiness. I sat quietly thinking that reticence would serve well on all occasions.

"After some time, all three of us left the house. I noticed a singular trait in Bharati. He would talk incessantly without letup. When he ceased talking, he would proceed to singing. Rarely did he keep quiet. It seemed he was unmindful of others in his company. He sang even as he walked.

"On our way, many greeted him respectfully. Bharati returned their greetings irrespective of the station they occupied in life. He would join his hands together, bring them closer to his face, and greet. He would not walk while greeting someone. He would cease walking, and then greet them. He would also talk to a few who conveyed their respects to him profusely.

"How Bharati, impoverished as he was, had earned so much reverence was not easily comprehensible then. It was highly doubtful that they had known to appreciate the magnificence of his poems. Be that as it may, he was revered as a guru.

"We reached Sankara Chettiar's house. Having left me in the pyol outside, they both went into the house. Within moments of their leaving, sleep took possession of me, and to this day, there is no way of knowing how I, an eager traveller to Puducherry, succumbed to it. I woke up only when Bharati patted me. We reached the third floor of Chettiar's house.

"Aurobindo was seated alone in a secluded corner there. We sat after paying our respects to him. No one began the conversation. Bharati came to my rescue.

"'Here is the patriot from Tamil Nadu,' he introduced me to Aurobindo.

"'Does he not know that an application to the government has to be made before entering Puducherry?' said one of the Bengalis and laughed. He was followed by others, except Bharati. I smiled sheepishly! But Bharati betrayed no emotion. He came down with a blast. 'Among slaves do the Bengalis score higher than the Tamils?' That gave me the guts to raise my head.

"Bharati was taller than Aurobindo. He was an introvert. So was Aurobindo. Bharati's words had the impact of the scent of a jasmine flower. The words of Aurobindo were like the broad petals of the red lotus flower. New ideas and descriptions came sparkling out of them. While Bharati would catch phrases circling in the sky, Aurobindo would dig them out from the treasure buried in the earth. Poetic richness pervaded their speech. Like Bharati, Aurobindo also broke into guffaws.

"With this let me cease the narration of my first meeting with Bharati and begin his life story. What do you say, Kesav?"

"I am all for it," he said.

3

'Circulating worn out tales amongst us
Can be of no benefit'

THIS WAS BHARATI'S *VEDIC SUTRA* (AN APHORISM FROM the Vedas) for the benefit of us and others. Hence, it is expedient to listen to his own words for a description of extraordinary events in his life. I had tried many a time to make him talk of his early life in the course of our conversations. He had adroitly scuttled them all, and instead spoke of other interesting matters. The nuggets of his life, collected by others, could hardly suffice as his biography.

Bharati wrote a serial story called *Chinna Sankaran Kathai* (Story of Sankaran the lad) in 'Gnana Banu' magazine published by Subramania Siva.[1] I remember to have seen seven of its installments. It was rumoured that before its serialization was completed, the manuscript, along with a few of his poems and documents, was stolen by a traitor, who handed them over to the secret police stationed in Puducherry. The story was originally thirty chapters long. If the Puducherry government had them in their possession, then by returning them they would have done Tamil literature a great favour. *Chinna Sankaran Kathai* was almost seen as Bharati's autobiography. Every line would trigger uncontrollable laughter when read.

Amongst those who could furnish proper details of Bharati's life, Mandayam Srinivasachariar is the foremost. He lives by Parthasarathy Temple in Triplicane, Chennai. Another such person is Duraisamy Iyer, a well-known lawyer in Chennai. He formerly occupied the old Palm Grove bungalow in Royapettah, and presently lives in Aurobindo Ashram in Puducherry. 'Lokopakari' magazine editor, Parali. Su. Nellaiyappar, might be in the know of some details.[2] Bharati's wife, Mrs. Chellammal, could give authentic details on Bharati's family life and other aspects. A teacher in Puducherry, Kanaga Subburathinam, with the pen name Bharatidasan, who has the talent to write poems like Bharati himself, could be a source for interesting pieces on him. Amirutha, alias Aravamuthu Iyengar, who lives in Aurobindo Ashram, can bring in humorous anecdotes on Bharati. Bharati's brother, Viswanatha

Iyer (B.A.L.T), can also provide some information. Bharati's lookalike Sankara Iyer (the son of Bharati's aunt), lives in Chennai and knew Bharati. Bharati also deeply loved him. Along with them, if we consult those who approached him with devotion and admiration, we can somewhat piece together a biography of Bharati. In the meantime, I shall attempt my version.

Subramania Bharati was born in 1882 in Ettayapuram in the Tirunelveli District. Ettayapuram was a big zamin,[3] and its ruler, the zamindar, had the title Raja. Bharati describes Ettayapuram as 'Kavundanur Samasthan', the princely state of Kavundanur, in his *Chinna Sankaran Kathai*. By birth, Bharati was a Smarta brahmin of the Kantara Manikka Brahasarna sect.

"The princely state was adorned by the poets Thodi Narayana Iyengar, Pallavi Subbaramayyan, and Kambaramayanam Muththiruluthevar, and was ruled by Atana Ramasamy Kavundar (all imaginary names given to real people), who was proud of his victories in rooster fighting." Bharati made his avatar here.

Bharati's father, Chinnasamy Iyer, was very close to the ruler; he could enter the palace at will. He was adept in mathematics. As mathematics was a favourite of his own and his ancestors, he wanted Bharati to be well-versed in that. He was well-trained in mechanics.

It was said that even then (some sixty years earlier) he had the skill to dismantle and assemble the machines made abroad.

The English poet Goldsmith was of the view that mathematics did not demand imaginative skills. They say that to activate machines, one does not need superior mental skills. Bharati's father wanted his son to be trained in both and earn abundant wealth. Alternatively he wanted his son to go abroad after finishing his education and return as a District Collector clad in a shirt and trousers. He himself taught Bharati at first and then monitored him. Whenever he called on his son to instruct him in *Kanakku* (mathematics), Bharati would instantaneously blurt out "kanakku, pinakku, vanakku, manakku and amanakku."*

He repeated likewise when it came to machines. He was not lacking in alliteration. His father was interested in teaching him mathematics with zeal and enthusiasm. He was afraid of his son's overt gamesmanship. When Bharati was staring at a mathematical sum, his father asked him "Why this *vizhi* (stare)?" Bharati went on

---

* *pinakku* (disagreement), *vanakku* (a meaningless word), *manakku* (another meaningless word), and *amanakku* (castor plant) in that order.

as usual. "Vizhi, pazhi, kuzhi, vazhi, pizhi, suzhi.* His father was afraid his son was losing his mental poise.

An affectionate father, Chinnasamy Iyer did not want to thrash his son, who had lost his mother quite early in his life. Bharati's physique was so thin that it raised doubts that there was any life left in him. He was fond of physical exercise all through his life. He said that he wanted to wrestle. If ever he found anyone doing exercises, he would sit before the person and imitate the actions, and made himself the laughing stock of his friends.

Bharati had no strong memory of his mother. He lamented that he lacked that experience. He longed for the motherly love that the neighbourhood children received from their mothers. His wistfulness for motherly love kept him a child all his life. For him, even a baby girl born only a day before was a mother. As you know, in his songs he repeatedly calls "Amma, Amma."

If a child in the street was known to be motherless, Bharati would be stunned. I could not fathom his feelings. "Oh man, is there no way of getting reprieve from my mother fixation?" he would ask his friend nearby, but a brief moment later he would croon "Amma, Amma." Bharati's father with his visible presence could

* "awake, blame, pit, path, wring, and whirl" in that order.

not make Bharati an accomplished mathematician like him, but Bharati's invisible mother succeeded in making him a poet.

As a boy, Bharati enjoyed more privileges in the Ettayapuram palace. Since he was close to the Samasthan, the Vidhwans and others loyal to the Samasthan showed him love and respect. Let there be no doubt among Tamil pundits of the fact that the title 'Bharati' was conferred on him by Vidhwans from the Samasthan.* Still, as a child, Bharati revealed his precocious intelligence through his retorts, to the bewilderment of others. As a young lad, he was seen as having the experience of a centenarian.

In the Ettayapuram court, when poets recited their works for official recognition, Bharati would be there as a participant and give vent to his frank opinions on them. Stung by his remarks, the Vidhwans would be left murmuring about whether to take him seriously.

Bharati received the friendship of important poets and the support of the Samasthan in abundant measure. He lived joyously like a honey-sucking beetle. With minimal reading he scored highly in his exams. He

* The title 'Bharati' a variant of the name Saraswathi, the Goddess of learning, was conferred on him at the age of eleven by Sivagnana Yogi, a Tamil savant, in the *Ettayapuram Samasthan*.

sang his songs that had no regard for obsolete rules of prosody. Since the Samasthan buoyed up in titillating verses, he too sang prurient songs in the same spirit. Had they been in circulation, they would have brought disrepute to Bharati, but luckily they vanished without trace. Bharati's oral compositions of verses on specific matters born at the insistence of his friends might have wafted along with the greater sound of the world.

His father died before Bharati came of age.

4

AFTER THE DEATH OF BHARATI'S MOTHER, HIS FATHER, Chinnasamy Iyer, married again. A son and a daughter were born of that marriage.[1] At that time, Bharati was a young Samasthan poet and his siblings were children. By the time he died, Chinnasamy Iyer had lost all his wealth in his earnest pursuit of installing machines in India. When the family was in dire straits, where was the question of sending Bharati to England for higher education? In our country, the common fate of ninety out of a hundred families was to totter pathetically after the head of the family met with a sudden demise. Even after granting that there existed fewer insurance companies then, it was still doubtful if Chinnasamy Iyer had paid any premiums to them. Knowing the kind of person that he was, we can conclude with certainty that he would have apportioned that sum only to the repair of his machines, if at all. Bharati often said that Chinnasamy Iyer clung to his pursuits firmly.

More or less around this time, Bharati got married. It can be said that he acquired the poet's poverty early in his life. Can anything be expected from a cow in abnormal situations, when it fails to produce milk even on regular occasions? The same can be said of Bharati's education under these trying times.

Bharati since his younger days would talk very humorously, and it was no wonder that the Raja of Ettayapuram developed a liking for him. But Bharati could not maintain his association with the Raja, who was attracted to erotic songs, for long.

Bharati showed early signs that he did not care for riches. We see people develop intimacy with those who are only nominally well-off, and even the wise heap praise on the inanities expressed by the rich, all to get their support for subsistence. In a milieu like that, it is no mean matter that Bharati did not care for the Raja's support.

In the Raja's company, Bharati acquired a bad habit. Out of concern for Bharati, who had a fragile physique, the Raja would exhort him humorously, "Brother! You shouldn't keep your health like this. You should eat well. It is good to consume *pooranathi lekiyam*[2] to improve digestion. You don't know the greatness of *pooranathi lekiyam*. If you take it, then you may eat all the food contained in a large vessel, and not only that, the vessel itself can be swallowed." He made Bharati fall into the habit of enjoying *pooranathi lekiyam*. Bharati used to give a humorous account of it when he was in a happy mood.

What the elders called *Ganga Paanam*, the drink, Bharati, even as a lad, renamed it as 'Ganja Paanam'* and got addicted to it.

Bharati's case was an example of how the poor could never benefit from their contact with the rich. Bharati's consumption of *pooranathi* for better health was similar to Gandhi's consumption of meat to strengthen his body, and his subsequent declaration to his unsuspecting mother that he had no appetite for supper. The recommendations given to both Bharati and Gandhi by the Raja and another person respectively were not out of ill will. However, we can learn from these incidents that such habits can be formed among the young due to misleading information. They are pointers in the direction that elders should be wary of the influence they might exert on the young.

---

* Ganja Paanam was Bharati's funny coinage for the juicy secretion that flows into one's mouth while consuming ganja, an intoxicating Indian hemp.

Disenchanted with Ettayapuram, Bharati left for his aunt's house in Benares. He prepared for Calcutta University's entrance examination, as Benares had no university of its own. He studied in the high school connected to Central Hindu College. He used to jocularly describe his days in the school thus:

"They ask you to read in the morning and in the evening. When I was a student I never read books. If I attended school in the morning then I would not attend in the evening. Thinking that I would attend in the evening, I would not attend in the morning and as an afterthought I would not go in the evening either. Morning and evening classes would get skipped. It is wrong to say that books decorate the hand. Silk shirts and emerald rings decorate the hand. I never carried a satchel to school. Instead I had just a few letters and a pencil in my pocket. I used to write funny remarks in prose and verse about the teacher in the classroom and pass them to the next boy, and we would laugh together. Then it would spread to the whole bench. Before the teacher found out what this noise was all about, I would sneak out of the classroom and reach home to watch the ever flowing Ganges from the upper storey. That was how I did my studies."

One should not reach the hasty conclusion that Bharati did not study anything based on what he said of himself in later years. He passed the entrance exams with a first class. He joined F.A. (Faculty of Arts), which was then the pre-university course, but due to either family problems or to his dislike of college studies, he bade it goodbye after a year.

How can kith and kin protect and nourish this boy with a wayward mind? They were all the more worried because he was not dumb, but was one who proved his intelligence by passing with a first class without much reading.

His success had a speciality. There was no subject in Tamil. But he qualified himself in two languages – English, which was, needless to say, compulsory, and Hindi, which he had learnt in two years. His Hindi pronunciation made everyone think that he belonged to Gosai brahmin sect of North India. There are certain phonetic sounds in Hindi which can be brought out from the stomach, which a Tamil would find difficult. But Bharati spoke well, and his Hindi diction was exemplary.

For whatever reason, Bharati did not like either Benares or his studies. The Raja of Ettayapuram wrote to Bharati to come back. Seizing it as an opportunity, he left for Ettayapuram and never returned to Benares. He could look forward to having no permanent job except the compassion offered by the palace. It need not be said that he himself had no money.

5

BEFORE HE LEFT FOR ETTAYAPURAM, BHARATI PUT AN end to his schooling, bid farewell to Benares, and took a final dip in the Ganges. The zamindar might have provided him for his journey. Bharati used to say that he left for Ettayapuram because of the letter he received from the zamindar.

The zamindar and Bharati were unique friends. When together they fought but when separated, they longed for each other's company – the kind of drama you can witness between on-screen lovers. The zamindar took pride in his power and riches, and in Bharati, for what he was. Each did not concede that the other was in any way superior.

The rich do not always reserve their benevolence for any single person or place for too long. Like a whirlwind, it rotates fast. The zamindar was longing for closeness and affection until he sighted Bharati, but when he did, he got reminded of himself as 'Raja'. Bharati had no work but he was paid a salary. Of that there are no records. So long as he was in the Raja's good books, he did not have to worry about his salary. But how long that would have lasted was anybody's guess.

Bharati had described the zamindar's indeterminate character well in *Chinna Sankaran Kathai*. He would give vague orders such as 'Give land to Rakka Pillai'. But then who was Rakka Pillai? Which land, and what was its extent? Was it cultivable land or uncultivable land, or a plot for constructing a house? The palace officials, afraid of approaching the zamindar for clarification, would dispense the orders according to their liking. Bharati said that they ran their own whimsical Darbar.

'How could I prolong in such a vacuous kingdom?' Bharati would ask his helpless companions. Bharati used to talk of such times whenever an occasion presented itself.

The Raja was fond of the book 'Koolappa Nayak's Love',[1] which he liked to have read aloud (this incident is mentioned in *Chinna Sankaran Kathai*). He derived exquisite pleasure from erotic poems and dance recitals. He pined for love and indulged in lengthy discussions about it. It was Bharati's fate that he had to listen to all of those. 'The Englishmen's rigid laws didn't scare and unnerve me as much as the Raja's prurient talks,' said Bharati often.

The Raja's erotic leanings, the unreliable support he extended, and the mean jealousies of co-workers forced a decision on Bharati, who held a job with no duties attached, had a family to care for and an independent mindset, to leave Ettayapuram.

Some may suspect that Bharati's mind was more unstable than the Raja's infirm mind. But such instances are common in the lives of worthy people. They used to shift from one job to another rapidly. Until they found something suitable for themselves, their turmoil would not cease.

Until Gandhi took to Satyagraha, his life was in turmoil. As long as Buddha could not realize his own self, the disquiet he went through was unbearable for him. The agony Vivekananda experienced until his mind found peace cannot be described in words. Swami Ramtirth shared a similar predicament. It is no wonder then that people who are on a spiritual quest have an unstable mind.

How to sustain himself without the Samasthan job was Bharati's concern. Bharati used to joke that unless the monkey left the branch it was holding tightly, it would not reach for another. If one were to ask 'What would happen if one left the present branch when there was no branch to cling on to?' Bharati would retort, 'He will have to fall down and die and there is no use in being afraid.' But Bharati did not share the fate of the monkey he used as an example.

There was a job vacancy for a Tamil teacher in Sethupathy High School in Madurai, the capital of the erstwhile Pondy Kingdom. Records are not available to confirm whether Bharati applied for it or if he got it through someone's recommendation.

It was said that there was only one trustworthy friend to Bharati in Ettayapuram until he found a job as a Tamil teacher. This friend was a Samasthan clerk, an Iyengar. Bharati used to shed tears whenever he remembered him. Bharati grieved over the fate of the clerk who was highly accomplished, and the extraordinary play that he wrote which never saw the light of day. We do not know anything of the young man, his whereabouts, and if he is still alive.

It is my guess that Bharati had accepted his job as a Tamil teacher in 1901 or 1902. He had left for Chennai before the end of 1903. It seems he continued on the job for one or one and a half years.*

---

* Bharati worked as a Tamil teacher in Madurai Sethupathy High School in Madurai for three months, from 1 August 1904 to 10 November 1904. He reached Chennai in the later part of November 1904.

Bharati had unique credentials for the Tamil teaching post. He had only the title 'Bharati' conferred on him by Samasthan scholars. He could not match the skills of Tamil pundits who could recite at will the sutras of 'Nannool' (a grammatical work). Though we can say that he might have seen the 'Nannool' book, it was doubtful if he had learnt it by rote.

'Insertion, elision, and omission are three changes in a letter that can occur first, middle, and last.'

Bharati used to ridicule this sutra in unimaginable ways. He did not like 'Nannool' at all. How Bharati with so much hatred for 'Nannool', could have served as a Tamil teacher is a matter of wonder.

Some of his students were overgrown. He was neither old nor strong in build. It could be said that his knowledge of grammar was nil. The place was also new. He must have been praying for ways to get out of that job. How could he have lived his life as a Tamil teacher?

At that juncture, the editor of 'Swadesamitran', the late Mr. Subramania Iyer, reached Madurai and was introduced to Bharati.[2] He immediately recognized Bharati's genius. He wanted to take him to Chennai by any means.

Subramania Iyer was a seer who awakened Tamils politically. He had no meanness about him. He requested Bharati to go with him to Chennai. We are not sure whether present day editors would show the same kind of courtesy to talented teachers as he did. The political services rendered by Iyer and the love he showed to Bharati would never be forgotten by Tamils. Here I had a doubt. What prompted Bharati to accept the journalist's vocation, a patriotic feeling or its attractive salary? I approached S. Duraisamy, a friend of Bharati since 1904, for clarification.

He said: "Feelings of patriotic devotion in our country were born due to the Bengal Partition. Bipin Chandra Pal's writings and oratory kindled our emotions. This was in 1905. But Bharati (he used to mention him plainly as 'Bharati' and not as 'Bharatiyar' due to his intimacy with him) developed in me strong feelings of nationalism. For Bharati, patriotism was not something he borrowed. He owned it. He personified Tamil Nadu in all its fullness." Can anyone say anything more of him?

6

BHARATI REACHED CHENNAI AT THE BEGINNING OF 1904.* While narrating his life, there could be some chronological errors. I inquired about them with knowledgeable people. They too harboured similar doubts. You might have experienced that certain words to which we seek meanings, are missing in dictionaries. My experience was similar to that.

He joined 'Swadesamitran' as an assistant editor, though for a meagre salary. But he had to work hard. "Bharati. You write Tamil well. You could be paid in lakhs. You are Kalidasa but I am not King Bhoja to pay you adequately," Subramania Iyer used to tell Bharati.

"He was an artful dodger in extracting work from me. But I got the expertise in journalism from him, and hence in a way I regard him as my guru," said Bharati.

---

* Bharati reached Chennai in November 1904.

He used to relate an incident often, and I will reproduce it exactly the way he told: "Before leaving for home in the evening, I would be waiting to approach him with the urgent need for money. A man would bring me a cup of coffee and say that Iyer had asked him to deliver it. When I would be thinking highly of Iyer's love for me, he would appear. I would quite forget to ask him for money."

"Bharati! Sir Henry Cotton had spoken so well of India in Britain. Did you know of it?" he would ask.

"Yes, I did," I would answer.

"It should be published in our paper tomorrow itself, should it not?"

"Of course. It should be."

"Who can translate his speech without impairing its substance but you?" He would ask. I would stand with a bowed head.

"But you don't have to translate it by staying in the office. You can leave now, do it at home, and bring it tomorrow morning. It will not take more than half an hour for you."

"I would take it home. Like the Taluk office clerk, I worked not only in the office but also at home. That is the fate of a wage earner. Iyer tricked me into doing the work. But do you know how translation work helped me? English is a nice language. Without defacing its content, I had to find suitable words in Tamil to convey it in an interesting way to Tamils. I understood the majesty and richness of Tamil even more clearly."

It may be surprising for us to know that Bharati worked as a translator in 'Swadesamitran', and enriched Tamil by infusing new life into Tamil words. Iyer never asked him to write editorials. Because of Bharati's extreme views on politics, he might not have been allowed to write. But he was not asked to write articles on other topics either.

Daily papers gave importance to scoops and foreign affairs. They were not intent on making readers question timeworn ideas and be valiant. They also lacked the time and resources to do that. Knowing fully well those shortcomings, Lokmanya Tilak ran his magazine 'Kesari' as a weekly until his death, despite many entreaties made to him to convert it into a daily. 'Kesari' (now published as a bimonthly) had transformed the minds of Maharashtrians. No other magazine could claim a similar reputation except Gandhi's 'Navjeevan'.

Bharati with his paltry salary could not find an independent house. In big cities, people like him could only share a portion of a house. Bharati had tellingly described the travails of such occupants in his highly imaginative work *Gnanaratham*. Bharati had humorously noted that a raise of a meagre one rupee in their salary would simultaneously bring an addition of two children to their household. It was an irony that made men grow philosophical.

During that time, many people, enamoured of his poetry, became close to Bharati. S. Duraisamy Iyer was foremost among them. He stood Bharati in good stead by helping him at all times, and melted in sorrow at the mention of his name. This is no occasion to talk of S. Duraisamy Iyer's munificence, his extraordinary brilliance, his humility, and his supreme love for Tamils.

'Do not take pride in your moustache. A murrel fish too has a long one, but it ends up being eaten. Do you sport it to become subservient to the ruling class?' roared Surendranath Arya, a Telugu man and Bharati's close friend. Like the Japanese, he had a diminutive build and his physique had the tautness of a jaggery cake. He had undergone a rigorous imprisonment for six years. Enthused by the affection shown by Danish priests, he became a Christian. He worked briefly for the Self-Respect Movement. He was full of vigour and enthusiasm.

Third on the list is our friend Mr. V. Sarkarai Chettiar, a devoted Christian who knew well the ideology of the National Movement. He had a great liking for substantive ideas and good literary works, though he did not have a firm mind. But he was always after big accomplishments. You might have known that he was defeated as a mayoral candidate in Chennai when he ran against an Englishman. He owed his defeat to the withdrawal of support by the Justice Party. But he became the Mayor of Chennai at a later date.

Mandayam S. N. Tirumalachariar was the fourth. He was rich, and died even before he turned thirty-five. He was energetic and strong in his physique. He squandered a large amount of his wealth before he died. He gave his money to 'India Weekly', that was run by Bharati. A relative of his, also a Tirumalachariar – M. P. Tirumalachariar to be exact – was a friend of Bharati. It was rumoured that he had married an English woman in Europe and his entry to India was barred owing to his involvement in a violent revolutionary movement.

Mandayam Srinivasachariar was another friend. He is a good man, and lives in Triplicane. On account of their connection with the Tuticorin Swadeshi Shipping Company, his family lost several lakhs of rupees.[1] He maintained a close friendship with Bharati for twenty years in Chennai and Puducherry. He was one of the proprietors of 'India'. He was well versed in several languages including Tamil, Kannada, Urdu, French and English.

Dr. M. C. Nanjunda Rao, a well-known physician, lived in Mylapore. A patriot and philanthropist, he was older than Bharati. All the help and guidance he gave to the troubled patriots cannot be adequately described. His friendship with Bharati was an eccentric one.

Bharati's laughter did not sound like an explosion. It was like a musical trill. Neither a bombastic one. Nor a grin. Smiles can be read. But Bharati's laughter could be heard as music. Nanjunda Rao was attracted to Bharati's laughter. He enjoyed Bharati's charm, purity, and wisdom, as shown in his face and laughter. Bharati lived for a while in George Town in Chennai. Nanjunda Rao forced him to relocate his residence to Triplicane when Thangammal, Bharati's daughter, fell ill with a fever. He wanted to be closer to Thangammal to take care of her. His love for Bharati could not be measured.

I will mention only one more friend. He was very senior to Bharati. Pronouncing his name might have intimidated the police. He was Krishnasamy Iyer, Deputy Commissioner of Police in Chennai, and a close friend of Justice Krishnasamy Iyer. It was not known how Bharati befriended him, a police official. No need to get startled by the friendship between the patriotic

Bharati and the government servant Krishnasamy Iyer. We can cite the example of the friendship between Gandhi and Dinabandhu Andrews. Individuals need not be blamed for their affiliation to groups which had good and bad traits.

7

BHARATI COULD NOT CONTINUE FOR LONG IN 'Swadesamitran'. He had written in his *Puthiya Aathichudi*, "Ask for the bigger than the biggest."[1] No wonder there was no space for his aspiration in 'Swadesamitran', which had no revolutionary leanings. It supported the policies and practices of the Congress party, that toed a moderate line in politics. Tilak infused a new spirit into Congress, and his expressions were found in some part in the Congress meeting held in Surat.

Viceroy Lord Curzon divided Bengal into Upper Bengal and Lower Bengal in 1906.* The Bengalis protested against this vehemently, which led to the struggle for Swaraj. The events that led to the partition and its aftermath were unbearable to Bharati. G. Subramania Iyer knew that if Bharati wrote of it, he

* Lord Curzon divided Bengal in 1905.

would go to prison. After reaching a consensus with Subramania Iyer, Bharati left 'Swadesamitran'. Iyer held his admiration for Bharati until the very end of his life. There was no basis for the rumour that Bharati left 'Swadesamitran' out of bitterness. G. Subramania Iyer was neither a moderate like Gokhale nor a revolutionary like Gandhi. Hence it was befitting that Bharati, with his extremely revolutionary mindset, left Iyer's office of his own accord.

Bharati didn't remain inactive after his stint at 'Swadesamitran'. He started a weekly Tamil publication named 'India' with the support of his friends. It is said that red is the sign of danger, but 'India' was printed on red paper. Though a weekly, it had a good circulation of four thousand copies. That was in 1906. Its special contents were: 1. News written boldly and fearlessly in an enchanting style. 2. Songs. 3. Cartoons. 4. Biographies of eminent people. From time to time, it also brought out research articles. Bharati's fame began to spread very soon after 'India' started its publication.

The Bengalis' protest against the partition of Bengal resulted in the publication of revolutionary journals like 'Navasakthi', 'Yugantharam', 'Vande Mataram', and 'New India'. The Swaraj feelings and slogans that originated in Bengal spread across the whole of India.

Though an old man, Dadabhai Naoroji, the president of Congress in Calcutta, boldly pronounced four important resolutions - Swadesh goods, the banning of foreign goods, national education, and Swaraj - were passed with a resoluteness that gave jitters to both the moderates and the government. The proceedings of the Calcutta Congress were responsible for the incarceration of patriots. Moderates supported the government. It was the norm that freedom fighters who did not align with the Moderates were sent to prison. Moderates with the backing of government were set on reversing the firm resolutions of the Calcutta Congress. Congress, that was hitherto only petitioning, had suddenly risen to questioning and this was seen as a worrisome prospect by the government.

In 'India', Bharati took forward the new policies of the Congress in his writings. Every week, new policies enthused the entire nation. At a time when older leaders in Chennai were afraid of inviting the Bengali stalwart Bipin Chandra Pal, Bharati and his friends brought him to Chennai. The five orations he delivered were treasures to Tamil politics. No bigwig consented to preside over Bipin Babu's first speech out of fear. Only G. Subramania Iyer saved the honour of Tamilians by consenting to preside. We can assume that it could have been due to the influence of Bharati on Iyer.

Gandhi was not the first to set foreign clothes ablaze. The first such fire broke out at Triplicane in Chennai, when Bipin Babu had come to speak. Costly alpaca coats and caps were burnt in hundreds. All of a sudden, political revolt began in Chennai. There was an organization called 'Mahajana Sabha' in Chennai, and its members paid obeisance to the government. Bharati established 'Chennai Jana Sangh'. Its activities from start to finish were looked upon with suspicion by the police.

Congress convened a meeting in Surat in 1907. By then, Bengal had witnessed bombings. It appeared that gunshots would soon be heard. The nation was in tumult. After Calcutta, the meeting was to be held in Nagpur. The Moderates of Nagpur were determined to water down the basic resolutions of the Calcutta meeting, but the majority of the Nagpur Congressmen gave no opportunity for such plans to be completed. The Moderates changed the meeting venue to their citadel in Surat (situated in Gujarat). The patriots were enraged, and assembled under the leadership of Lokmanya Tilak. Tilak's group stood firm that the resolutions should not be altered in any manner. To lend him support, Bharati, V.O. Chidambaram Pillai, and many others, comprising a group of a hundred representatives, went to Surat.

It is all too well-known that at the Surat meeting, the Moderate Surendranth Bannerjee was pelted with chappals. Chairs were broken and there were fisticuffs, and ultimately the meeting did not take place. It was said that Congress was divided in Surat because of the militant intervention of Tamils. Why shouldn't the Tamils take pride if the divide had benefitted the nation?

But S. Duraisamy Iyer said it did not take place at the behest of Tamils. He had gone to Surat with Bharati. Iyer said that Bharati regaled the Tamil representatives on the train journey. Could there be any chance for less enjoyment in Bharati's company?

We shall conclude this chapter with a mention of an event. Bharati had not seen Tilak until the meeting took place in Surat. He desired to see him. It was raining in Surat when the Congress met. There was a lack of proper thoroughfare between the meeting shed and where the representatives were staying. The repaired path was also damaged due to rain. Tilak was restoring the path with some men. No work was too big or too small for that great man. Bharati, triggered by the desire to see Tilak, went out and enquired but no one knew his whereabouts. Saddened, Bharati walked on aimlessly along the path that led to the Congress meeting area. He saw about a hundred people engaged in the restoration work. He approached the supervisor monitoring the work with an umbrella in his hand. What happened next was related thus by Bharati to me.

"I saw the back of the umbrella. I went in front of him and met his eyes. They shone on me like fireballs emitting heat. Without a word, I touched his feet and prostrated myself before him."

It was hard not to be deeply devoted to him after seeing Lokmanya's fiery eyes. Was there any surprise that his eyes sparkled with divine power and a thirst for independence?

8

THE YEAR 1905 WAS IMPORTANT IN THE HISTORY of India. Indians woke up from their slothful slumber.

Patriotism had taken a new turn since 1907.

Lokmanya Tilak and the Partition of Bengal were responsible for those changes. The hardships undergone by Indians prior to 1906 did not boost the morale of the public.

The hardships we undergo are of two kinds; one is what happens to us on its own, the other is due to what we bring upon ourselves. The bullock pulling carts suffers. The bull that fights another bull also suffers. But the former, in doing its chores, loses independence and self-esteem, the qualities that develop in the character of the latter are on account of the fight. Man cannot accomplish any task while fearing hardship. Sustaining hardship leads to the attainment of fame. Hardship gives man fame, responsibility, and happiness.

Besides the dissolution of Congress in Surat,

another event took place. Lala Lajpat Rai and Sardar Ajit Singh were deported from Punjab to Burma in 1906.[1] *Lajapatiyin Pralabam* (Lajpat's lament) was sung by Bharati on that occasion. Tilak and his group wanted Lajpat to head Congress in 1907. Moderates afraid of the government did not accede to the demand. Lajpat, after his release, reached the Congress meeting in Surat. He was drawn to Tilak for his ideology and had a liking for the Moderate Gokhale. He tried hard to unite them, but that never happened. At that time, John Morley was Secretary of State for India and Lord Minto was Viceroy of India. Morley had telegraphed the Viceroy to accommodate the Moderates. A few, including Gokhale, knew of that.

Gokhale sent word to Tilak through Lajpat that the government would surely imprison those who opposed the Moderates. Aurobindo was consulted by Tilak. Aurobindo's narration of the entire episode, when heard, would surely chill the listener. Tilak knew he was inviting trouble by not following the path of the Moderates. But the stand he took brought a fundamental change in the attitude of the people of our country. Bharati was one of the notable men who welcomed it wholeheartedly. Those events served basically to determine Bharati's life. Bharati, as a great poet, might have stayed away from politics like poet Rabindranath Tagore. It could be said that he chose otherwise due to the influences of Tilak, Aurobindo, and Bipin Babu.

Upon his return to Chennai from Surat, Bharati wrote fiercely in support of Tilak's views and his approaches in 'India'. Tilak was sentenced to six years of rigorous imprisonment in 1908. The government began the task of felling the 'giant trees' that stood supporting Tilak and his group, one after another. After the first blow was dealt by the government, people began guessing who would be axed next. The government in Chennai did not like Bharati's 'India' .

The first arrow was shot at the publisher of 'India'. Bharati's friends knew that the next arrow would be aimed at Bharati. It was a very trying situation in Bharati's life. His friends thought that Bharati should not be sent to prison under those circumstances. He had acquired prominence both as a patriot and as a poet. His literary friends contended that Bharati should serve the muse rather than languish in prison. I have a good reason to elaborate on this. Some without inside knowledge thought of him as a coward and chicken-hearted. Some openly said so. Bharati was neither. A man's speech reveals his state of mind. In Bharati's writings, no one can detect traces of fear and leniency. I shall later relate an incident to show that he was not the person to be put down by intimidating circumstances.

Bharati went to Puducherry, acting upon the advice of his friends. This need not be described in detail. Bharati placed great faith in his friends' counsel. They ruled in favour of Bharati's poetic contribution to the nation. A man faces dilemmas in these ways: duty will be seen in two dimensions, each unrelated to the other, and choosing between the two is the real dilemma.

The troubles Bharati went through were far more excruciating than what he would have undergone in imprisonment. It was akin to jumping out of the frying pan into the fire. Bharati reached Puducherry in 1908. Puducherry was a dangerous place. It was one of the small regions in India under French rule. After the Franco-German war in 1870, the French were relegated to the condition of depending on the British. Hence the Puducherry overlords positioned themselves as subordinate to the British Indian government in anticipation of its favours.

In those times, there were no popular leaders in Puducherry. The people were also steeped in French culture and they were relatively free. Under such circumstances, how could one expect them to appreciate Bharati's poems? In the beginning, some of the Puducherry citizens without qualms derided Bharati for being a fugitive. Was this not reason enough to avoid extending help to Bharati? Others saw him as a rebel against the powerful state and became afraid. What kind of help could Bharati have expected from them? The place was new and he was with little means. Additionally, he had antagonized the government. Naturally Bharati could not hope to roll on a bed of roses. Initially, he took a position as a boarder in Iyengar's house, adjoining Eswaran Dharmaraja Koil Street. As a stranger, Bharati found it hard to find someone to converse with in Puducherry. If someone took asylum in Puducherry without solvent means, he would be uncared for. He would be counted as one among the unknown multitudes.

People looked askance at Bharati as they came to know of him, little by little. If someone occupied a seat on the bench on the iron bridge at the beach, he would vacate it soon after catching sight of Bharati approaching. It was not out of respect but out of fear of his identity. That was more degrading than solitary confinement. What would be the state of a hungry man who is not able to eat anything when he is provided with many varieties of delicious foods? What can be said of so many people living beside Bharati but not able to benefit from him?

Not that everyone should be a hero. But does that mean that others should live as cowards instead? Is there any limit for being fearful? Of course there can be a limit to being afraid for the people of Puducherry. Though Puducherry is under French rule the subjects are Indians – Tamils. If limits are not set for these people who are fearful by nature, will not their grace turn into disgrace?

Mandayam Srinivasachariar joined Bharati in Puducherry soon after. The patriots wanted 'India' to resume its publication from Puducherry. Printing machines arrived from Chennai. 'India' began its republication from a rented building at Rue Dupleix. The Indian government issued a warrant against him. Do you know which among his writings that appeared in 'India' earned him a warrant? 'When will this thirst for freedom abate? When will our infatuation for slavery die?' These very lines of Bharati, chanted like Krishna's hymns, were responsible, I do remember.

"Give me cows. Give me health. Bless me and my family to attain prosperity. When will I ever see the petals of your feet? Save me from Yama's assistants." Prayers like these were the stuff of old yarns, of primitive scriptures. They would be viewed as normal by the people and even the government. Who would take cognizance of prayers said mutely for the welfare of the self and the family? But when Bharati said "Our infatuation for slavery", would it not annoy the public and the government? They would raise the question, "How could Bharati talk of 'our infatuation for slavery"?' The government knew that unless people were duped into newer ways of cheating, governing them would be hard. They could not be unmindful of Bharati's virulent speech and his poetic creations, which were full of life.

But for how long could 'India' get published from Puducherry? If the fear of the people and the wrath of the government get together, a good journal will fold up fast. It may be forced to take its own life. 'India' exuded the charm of clandestine love. But would it last long? It would retain its spirit and craze only until it was made public. Once their identity was made public, the majority of lovers would not have the grit to withstand the vicissitudes of its outcome. Patriotism too would resemble clandestine love, for it would march on the royal path until the government intimidated it. All the patriots, until they undergo hardship, will 'shout' Vande Mataram. It is inappropriate here to use the word 'chant'.

This 'clandestine love', namely patriotism, was behind the response for 'India' when Bharati was publishing it in Puducherry. Its Tamil readers would not read it in public. 'India' was accorded the respect given to a confiscated book. Man does not die of danger, but he almost dies by the fear of it. 'India's life was shortened when people began to be afraid that the government from Chennai would stop its publication from Puducherry. 'The wish is the father of the thought,' is an English proverb that means 'a wish is the root cause of all thoughts'. Wish generates thoughts. Fear generates trouble. It can be said that fear is the mother of all troubles.

Before 'India' was stopped, those behind it (including Bharati) were subjected to untold miseries. Good deeds suffer due to a shortage of money everywhere. But in our country, it exceeds all limits. One who impersonates a dog should also bark. Those who witness it will give a certificate, but will not reward him with money. Most of the patriots were the have-nots. How would they have money? They should be ready to go anywhere from prison to the gallows. In between, they have to toil for sustenance. All this need not be told in detail to those endowed with imagination and patriotism.

The journal 'India' could not reach outside

Puducherry. Money that was owed to 'India' could not reach its office. There were also minor problems with the postal services. In sum, Bharati lost his means for living. Other workers in the office also faced difficulties. All were put through unimaginable hardships.

Valluvar[2] said, "Effort will result in good deeds." Instead of 'effort' I suggest the use of the word 'fervour', the illimitable energy source of patriots. To carry forward 'India', Bharati and his friends were triggered by the gift of 'fervour'. You may think lightly that running a magazine is an easy job when done with money. It is similar to waiting for the waves to subside before taking a bath. It is a futile, vedantic idea to ask patriots to first get rich and then work for the country's freedom.

Bharati shifted to Vilakkennai Chettiar's house on Eswaran Dharmaraja Koil street even before the closure of 'India'. I did not know Chettiar's original name. It was no doubt the same as when 'Adi Dravida' became meaningless after Gandhi lovingly coined the term 'Harijan.' It was a wonder that Chettiar never asked for the six months' rent, but silently listened to Bharati's songs and left. The house saved Bharati from ruin. It was used as the place for soiree, asylum, free food, and wise talk, with Bharati presiding over it undisputed.

I remember Aurobindo reached Puducherry in 1910. After he was released from the Maniktala dynamite case, he ran the 'Karmayogin' magazine and came out with forty issues. Bharati followed in his footsteps and edited 'Karmayogi', that was printed legibly and without errors at Saigon Chinnaiah's[3] press in Puducherry.

9

WHEN BHARATI STARTED 'KARMAYOGI' (IN 1910), THERE was political unrest across the whole of India.

Lokmanya Tilak was taken to Burma for a six year jail sentence. The government adopted a two- pronged approach. It used its right arm to suppress rebellion, and its left arm to bring forth reforms. This dual approach was called Minto-Morley Reforms. Morley vociferously stated from England that through those reforms, representatives to States would swell in large numbers. Aurobindo explained clearly in his 'Karmayogin' that it was not to be. He had stated that the people's representatives would only have the choice to raise questions, and they would not be replied to by the representatives of the government. Taught by twenty years of experience, the people realized that this was true.

The patriots had the occasion to point out that what Morley had said of the minor reforms would stand in the way of major reforms. Bharati made use of that occasion, and his 'Karmayogi' was in full swing in its operation. Swami Vivekananda had translated 'Patanjali's Yoga Sutra' into English. Bharati was of the opinion that there were discrepancies between the text and the translation. Hence, he translated it into Tamil from the original text and published it in parts in 'Karmayogi'.

Translation is always a heavy task. Without understanding the mind of the author, translating a work word for word is a schoolboyish activity. I well remember that Bharati's translation was appreciated by Aurobindo and other elders. Translations of the Mahabharata done by Griffith, an Englishman, and Romesh Chunder Dutt, a Bengali, were viewed as insipid by Aurobindo, Bharati and Va.Ve.Su. Iyer. Why do we elaborate on translation risking tediousness to our readers? It is to emphasize the importance of inner substance and the mentality that leads to it, rather than to its external aspects. Wise people understand it, but others get duped by what they see externally.

Bharati was not only a poet. He was extremely fond of philosophical discourse. The poem 'Sol Vendum' (A word is Needed) illustrates his philosophical quest. He needed a word to unlock nature's mysteries, and that would limitlessly benefit Tamils and others.

After the publication work stopped, hunger began to rear its ghastly head. During times of poverty, the wise and the do-gooders have to surrender to Valluvar. Valluvar said, 'When there is no food for the ear, feed something to your stomach.' But it appears that we have to change it by saying, 'When there is nothing for the stomach, continue to feed the ear a little longer.' Do not think that I go on philosophising mindlessly. This is not philosophy. Should not we be aware of the troubles the wise and the brave undergo in a country that is not liberated?

We are all neither wise nor brave. It is largely untrue to say that wisdom is born. Similar to the burgeoning of agarwood from cactus, revelation will arise from follies made.

Aurobindo was not provided with a bungalow to stay in immediately on his arrival. He and his disciples had occupied the third storey of a house belonging to Kalavai Sankara Chettiar. In the evenings, Bharati and his group visited and conversed with them.

I had good contacts with Indian leaders of those times. I also maintained some contact with leaders who arrived on the scene after the start of the Satyagraha

Movement. I knew Gandhiji too. But, in my view, none could excel Aurobindo and Bharati in conversational skills. Perhaps Gandhiji and Khaparde.[1] I am not sure.

There was substance and energy in Tilak's dialogues, but they were not smooth, humorous, or delightful. Khaparde's speech had great humour and elegance. Surendranath's speech was oration itself. Bipin Chandra Pal's speech was a mixture of bitterness and joy, but was also energetic and modern. Gokhale's speech was slender like a golden thread. Prasho Mehta was a thunder. Lajpat Rai spoke with discretion and poise. G. Subramania Iyer spoke with elaborate details. Salem Vijayaraghavachariar would not speak without legal and historical quotes.

The conversations of Bharati and Aurobindo had all the nine rasas. They sparkled with poetry, history, philosophy, experience, imagination, humour, jibes, explanations, desires to expound truth, abundant literary flavour, and limitless exultation. I regret that I had not learnt shorthand then. All I remember of them are some passages in conversations and remarks. I was not in the habit of diarising daily activities. Too much was lost. What can be done now?

Possibly there was none to match Va.Ve.Su. Iyer in his voracious readings of biographies of heroes, literature, books on warfare, Tamil classics, and writings of scholars from other countries. Iyer was fond of physical exercises like swimming and running. Bharati liked them but never did anything himself. He used to watch them with enthusiastic delight. He would bend his body involuntarily the way Va.Ve.Su. Iyer would during exercise. His heart would melt like wax without any serious thought. This can be classified as poetic emotion. This was the mind of love. Time would fly when Iyer, Bharati, and Srinivasachariar converged at Aurobindo's house and talked. If they began talking at four in the evening they would continue until ten at night with no thought of food.

It would appear that difficult tasks could be done with ease in their company. The confidence they exuded could shake a mountain. If you calculate profit and loss in activities, then there would not be liberty and history. Unless you plunge headlong into deep waters with confidence, the object lying underneath cannot be brought forth.

10

BHARATI WAS CHARMING TO LOOK AT. HIS COMPLEXION was good and he stood slightly taller than five and a half feet. His nose was attractive and it figured well on his majestic face. It was not like the eagle beak of Caesar or Rajagopalachariar. Caesar's nose rose in the middle and turned sharp at the end, ready to peck the passersby. Bharati's nose was long and well-shaped, without a speck of ugliness. Bharati's lotus eyes were lined with red. Under his eye lashes, his eyes would sparkle like fireballs. They were always pleasing to look at.

He had a broad forehead. His hair receded on both sides above his forehead like a sea that had burrowed into the land. A strand of hair stood on the middle of his scalp. The arrangement of his hair in this way made him attractive beyond description. He was more than half bald. His earnest attempts to cover his baldness, by bringing his hair together from both ends of his forehead, would provoke children to laugh. He would spend more than half an hour on this every day, and would present a different look each day.

Bharati sported a clean moustache. It was neither sharp like Kaiser's nor a neatly scissored one. It grew beautifully and daringly of its own accord. When not writing, his right hand would be stroking his moustache as if he was giving it a drill, but without twisting it. He sometimes wore a beard. But he was simply moustachioed for the most part of his life. As far as my memory goes, he was without a moustache only once. He was always very particular in having a bindi (a saffron dot) in the shape of a full moon on the middle of his forehead.

He would wrap a dhoti flatly around his waist. Mostly, he would not use an *angavastram*, for he was bored of it. He would wear a baniyan and a shirt. I had not seen him giving his dhotis and shirts for laundry. Either his acolytes or the housemaid would have washed them and kept them dry. The shirt over his *baniyan* (vest) might have been torn and buttonless. Over this he wore a coat with only a single button fastened for appearance sake.

On the left side of the buttonhole, he would insert a flower – a rose or a jasmine bunch, or in their absence any new fragrant flower, including neem flowers. A 'flower of the day' would be invariably inserted in the buttonhole of his shirt. In his left hand one could find a notebook, a few papers, and a book, and a Perumal Chetty brand pencil in his coat pocket. He always used pencil; and I never saw him write with a pen. Perhaps the fountain pen did not find its way into his pocket.

His handwriting was bold, each letter separate. Many of us join letters illegibly when we write, but not Bharati. He would put a dot on consonants as one would put a sandal dot on one's forehead. Children who knew only letters could read his handwriting. He would provide spaces between each line and allow margins on both sides of the paper.

A detail has been left out about his dress. He was fond of wearing a turban like the Sikhs. With that headgear, if he spoke in Hindi none would mistake him for a Tamilian, since his diction was flawless. He needed all these accoutrements on him before he ventured out. Beside them his girlish laughter resonated exceedingly like musical trills.

He could not put his left foot down with ease. There was a corn the size of a big coin on the sole of his left foot. If by chance he happened to press his left foot against any hard object he would sit down there itself, writhing in pain.

Bharati never stopped while walking. He would

often tell youngsters, "Don't stop, Don't stop". Bharati liked to walk while singing with his emaciated chest thrusting forward like a soldier. He would sing the French military marches 'La Marseillaise' and 'Sambre et Meuse' and stride appropriately to their beats. He used to say that he wanted to write many Tamil songs to suit those tunes. He did write a few in that genre.

Bharati always had a crowd - at least four or five people - around him. Even usurers would not attract people like him. A few would follow him in the street. Need it be mentioned that the secret police followed him at a distance?

When Bharati walked on the streets of Puducherry, people sitting on the *pyols* in front of their houses would rise up and bow to him. In turn, Bharati would bow and enquire about their wellbeing, before taking leave of them. Those who had been to Puducherry should be familiar with pushcarts.[1] They were not rickshaws. Some pushcarts had four wheels and those with three wheels had one in front. Those men, who pushed the cart from the rear, mostly belonged to the Harijan community. The pushcart drivers would be happy to see Bharati on the street. They would position the vehicle in front of him. They would not allow him to walk ahead and they would not demand fare from him either. They would refuse to be paid by him on arrival.

"Why pay us in coins?" the driver would ask.

"Do you want rupees?" Bharati would laughingly ask him.

"Why rupees?" he would refuse again.

All he wanted was clothes to wear and Bharati knew that. He would indulge in wordplay until the cart driver openly came forward with his demand for clothes. Then Bharati would give away whatever he was wearing. Whether the material was silk or a zari dupatta or worse, a torn shirt, all that was determined by the luck of the cart driver.

If any friend of his had gifted Bharati an *angavastram* because he did not have one, then it would perhaps end up with such a person. Pushcart drivers belonging to the area of Bharati's residence were fortunate. He loved the poor and the Harijans immensely. Bharati's mind would be engrossed in great ideas as he walked on the streets. They would come out sparkling all of a sudden. One morning, we were proceeding to Srinivasachariar's house. He was beautifully explaining the greatness of French literature and Victor Hugo's genius to me, when he heard a boy, sitting on the *pyol* in front of his house, read loudly, *Ilamiyil Kal* (Learn when you are young).

Pat came Bharati's retort, *Mudumayil Mann* (Get ruined when you are old).*

I was startled by his adroitness. Bharati said, "It seems you lack in logical reasoning. If someone is stony in his head then surely he is bound to be reduced to mud. That was how our ancestors had lived for two thousand years. We fear and tremble over everything. We should make our children sparkle like rays of sun so that they will not meet with ruin when they become old. They will be respected by the present and succeeding generations. If we fail to do that then we will be judged ill by them in future."

---

* Bharati, in his playfulness, punned on the Tamil words 'kal' and 'mann' . When the boy used the word 'kal' denoting 'learning', it is a verb, but 'kal' also means 'stone', which is a noun. Bharati shifted to the noun usage. The word 'mann' means mud and Bharati used it metaphorically to mean 'ruin'. Bharati quibbled on what the boy read from the book: 'If you are a stone (kal) when you are young, you are ruined (mann) when you turn old'.

11

I THINK THE SWADESHI SHIPPING COMPANY WAS established in 1909.* The stalwart patriot Sri V.O. Chidambaram Pillai was its backbone. The English merchants thought it was floated as a competitor to the B.I.S.N.C. (British India Steam Navigation Company), an English company. Even after the B.I.S.N.C. reduced its fares considerably, Indians neither boarded it nor loaded their cargo in it. Excited by this, Bharati spoke like a rishi bestowing a boon: "Our people have become wise. Henceforth they will have no disadvantages." Soon after, Chidambaram Pillai went to prison and the shipping company collapsed due to misdeeds of the British – all these are old stories. The company landed in a dilemma about the disposal of Koyalando, the only vessel left in its possession. It was sold to the B.I.S.N.C., the company which was responsible for its downfall. I

* It had been registered in 1906.

am not sure of it, but it may have been in 1913, the sale was negotiated through a Puducherry State Assembly member, a Bengali based in Chandannagar, a town to the west of Calcutta. When Bharati spoke of it he was filled with anger and grief.

"Are they thinking that by selling the company for a sum of fifty thousand rupees, they can wipe out the debts of this country? Shameless idiots! Instead they could have smashed the ship into smithereens and made them float on the sea. Our country can bear the loss. Self-esteem is paramount." He spoke agitatedly.

In his song '*Nadippu Swadeshigal*' (Pseudo Patriots), he had given great emphasis to self-esteem. He never grew weary of saying that it was greater than life. "A man without self-esteem would never grow," he would often say.

In the meantime, Neelakanda Brahmachari came to Puducherry. I do not know how he became acquainted with Bharati. Later on, he was listed in the government documents as the main accused in the Tirunelveli Conspiracy case (i.e. the Collector Ashe murder case). His complexion was as dark as coal. He ran the magazine 'Suryothayam' in Puducherry. Bharati supported him by sending his articles to that magazine. We, the disciples and friends of Bharati, argued with him. "Why don't you write to 'Swadesamitran', your old paper?" Bharati would agree to write, but in the end he would categorically refuse.

We had devotion and love for him. But still his response was unsatisfying. We raised it again. "You are children. You don't know the matter. 'Swadesamitran' is a paper of bygone times. It can't afford to sully its image by publishing Bharati," he said and laughed. We did not buy this mischievous excuse. But, without giving further room for discussion, he said, "'Swadesamitran' and I are opposed ideologically. It would be unfair to ask them to publish my writings. Besides the print magazines survive precariously. Since I am under the British government's scanner, it would pounce on the paper for publishing my writings. As of now, it is the only paper that has a steady run. Why should it court danger on my account?" As though he would not be calmed until he spoke on behalf of the managers of 'Swadesamitran', one among us who was known for his impertinence asked, "Did they ask you to write?" Bharati would engage anyone directly and correct him. But he would not speak ill of anyone in their absence.

"It is wrong to accuse them. Bharati is your elder. But he doesn't have to be an elder to them. You are all ignorant children."

We were somewhat satisfied by that reply. Though he spoke in support of the managers of 'Swadesamitran', his grouse against them came out somewhat. We repented for raising the issue with him.

During the years 1910-1911, Bharati's fame was not widespread. He was known as a rebel against the State. As it was difficult to separate his political activities from his poetic abilities during those times, there was no need to complain that a proper evaluation of him as a poet did not take place. It took nearly forty years to recognize the talent of the French writer Romain Rolland. Hence people could not be faulted for not understanding the worthiness of Bharati during the years 1905-1910.

In Chennai there was an English daily publication called 'Standard', edited by Ramashesaiya. Annie Besant ran it after renaming it 'New India'. In that, a discussion on Advaita philosophy took place between Bharati and Professor Sundara Rama Iyer. They had a difference of opinion on that. Sundara Rama Iyer was well versed in the *sastras* (sacred scriptures) but Bharati lacked knowledge of them. We would await the paper to read their arguments against each other. Sundara Rama Iyer was backed by his scholarly knowledge. Bharati was fortified by his keen intellectual fervour. What would be the outcome if these two Titans warred against each other? Only a warrior can know the might of another warrior. Bharati easily grasped the philosophy of Sage Sankara.

Bharati's idea that anyone can attain godliness was lampooned by Iyer. Everything was God, held Ramaiyar, which Bharati called a shallow philosophy. Since we were enamoured of Bharati, we thought he was right without hesitation. But we were reaffirmed in our decision when we discussed it in a tranquil mood. Aurobindo said that Sundara Rama Iyer lacked experience. "Philosophy cannot be understood by argument. It has to be experienced," he said.

By and large the pundits were deficient in experience, and they tried to judge great truths through their inefficient yardsticks. What is the difference between Gokhale, the moderate, and Lokmanya Tilak? Gokhale's knowledge of history, economics, literature, and oration was incomparable. But it was Tilak who stirred the emotions of the people and united them powerfully. Is there any need for the critic to be a creative writer? Gokhale was the servant of nature, and Tilak, its son. Did his landlord, who had read too many scriptures, know of the spirit of the Almighty equally well as Nandanar? Finally, the landlord had to kowtow to Nandanar. From whom did Ramanujan, the mathematical wizard, learn mathematics? It took a long time for Hardy to grasp the intricate works of Ramanujan. The child knows from where the milk comes. But, for others, only the arguments on milk are needed.

Sundara Rama Iyer extolled Bharati's mastery of English but he did not agree with his ideas. The same person had also castigated the essays on Gita by Aurobindo. Conducting arguments and counter arguments are the leisure activities of the pundits. Finding the truth and in its quest even sacrificing life are the duties of great people.

12

MUTHIYALPET IS AT A DISTANCE OF ONE MILE TO THE north of Puducherry. A twenty-year-old man called Krishnasamy Chettiar lived there. He was short and stout. Since his physique was firm, he was fondly called *Vellachchu* (Jaggery cake) Chettiar by Bharati. He was never weary in body and mind. Weaving was his profession. He was also well-off. He additionally had a clothing business. He used to visit Bharati often. After addressing Bharati as 'Swami', he would keep quiet for the rest of the time. Bharati liked him much and he used to sing his songs before him. Chettiar showed no signs of any literary taste. Some of us used to think that Bharati was wasting time on him. But he would laugh at the right moment, even ahead of us. Also, during the narration of tragic episodes, it would be hard to look at his melting face. Bharati would cite Krishnasamy Chettiar as an example of the perils of pre-judging anybody by appearance alone. "Who knows what species of snakes would dwell in which anthill?" Bharati would conclude later.

On occasions like that, Bharati would narrate stories. One of them, a short story, would appear to taunt Chettiar and applaud him at the same time. It is an old story that has to be retold because Bharati set it on Chettiar.

Two men, one a Chettiar and another a farmer, were walking in a forest area known for instances of robbery. They had set out early in order to reach their destination before dark. But it so happened that they entered the forest only after sunset. Bharati would ask Chettiar if the robbers could enter at this point of the story or later. To this Chettiar would reply that nothing would bother him since he was a 'Chetti' accompanying Bharati. Bharati would give a hearty laugh and we would join him. The robbers pummelled the farmer and took away his belongings. On seeing that, Chettiar (in the story of course), lay motionless. They patted him with a stick and then declared that he had become a lifeless log. Chettiar asked them if a log in their house would have ten rupees on it.

"What Chettiar! Is the story right?" Bharati asked.

"Whatever the story it ended only thus," said Chettiar and gave Bharati a ten rupee note.

"In the story they were robbers in the night. But I am a daylight robber," said Bharati and laughed. That would give Chettiar immeasurable happiness. He would fix his gaze on him with great admiration. I had seen no one as devoted to Bharati as Chettiar. He would appear to be an innocent man. But he gave a fine touch to Bharati's story and gave the money knowing Bharati's condition. But one had to be careful when giving money to Bharati. It is true he was without money, but anyone offering it as charity would be in trouble.

"Dash and trample on them dear child,
Spit on their face dear child"

You may have read the above and similar lines in his *Pappa Pattu* (Song for the Child). Anyone with the thought of giving alms to Bharati would get the treatment mentioned in the aforesaid lines. His face would be terrible to look at, with his eyes emitting fire and his moustache twirling. "Am I poor? Is hc the Lord of a charitable choultry?" He would be seething with anger.

No one could give alms to him. With due respect, one could pay his dues. Was he not an emperor of verse? His subjects could pay him their tax but he was no beggar to receive coins thrown at him. I remember a true story on this occasion. Samuel Johnson, the English author, was a noble man. He was very munificent, but lived a life of abject poverty. Unable to see him in that condition, a friend wanted to help him. He found Johnson's shoes in an irreparable state and replaced them with a new pair while he was asleep. When he awoke, Johnson found the new shoes before him. Angered by this misplaced act of benevolence, he hung them above the entrance of the room with a note attached to them:

"Whoever did this stealthily deserves to be beaten by the same shoes."

The shoes disappeared the following day. Many of us might think that Johnson was needlessly indignant. But I wish to retort, "Because of that thinking we remain slaves ourselves." But what would the retort bring in these circumstances? All those who were close to Bharati knew of his attitude towards money. He would never solicit it from strangers. It would also be unbearable to him if money did not come from known quarters.

Once, when his household ran out of victuals, Bharati wrote to a friend asking for a sum of five rupees. The letter received no reply. Bharati saw him in the evening.

'Bharati. I would have sent you the money. But it would have made you complacent and robbed your poetic sharpness from you. I didn't want it to happen.'

Bharati, when heard the explanation, got terribly angry. "Stop your bragging. Is poverty not enough for an intellectual? Should he also be ridiculed for it? You cannot be reformed. This country needs a revolutionary philosophy to crush it altogether," Bharati blasted him and left the place. Those who dared to insult the indigence of the poets are scum who would never understand the true nature of emotions. "Time will roll out. But words will stay," is an adage. If we compare our actions for subsistence with what Bharati and Johnson did, then we would know their eminence.

Bharati liked to treat his friends in the evenings. He would hold out some currency and ask them to check if it had exchange value. If it was declared in the negative, the ever resourceful Krishnasamy Chettiar would step in with his money to meet the occasion. Chettiar owned a garden near Muthialpet. It was the site of the *Kuyil* (Koel) song penned by Bharati. A miracle took place there. More about that later.

13

HUMAN BEINGS WANT TO GO FROM PLACE TO PLACE. To stay put in one place is like imprisonment. They want to stretch their legs to avoid numbness, walk briskly, have good blood circulation, see various places, hear different sounds, and experience new feelings. Money also needs to change hands, lest it becomes 'numb' too. Bharati's stay in Puducherry was like a prison for him. How long could he spend time there with the same set of people? Indian patriots were debarred from participating in Puducherry politics. How could they with pulsating energy keep quiet? That diktat dampened their spirits.

Rather than complaining unnecessarily, observing *mauna viratham* (a vow of silence) was preferable, said a learned one which was true. Unguarded words would bring disrespect to ideals. For the uncultured, altruism means a practice of trickery. So also their mean ideas formed about poetry and liberation. But the learned shall propagate their ideas, seek recourse in nature, and keep quiet, all to avoid despair. Bharati did all these things. He lived in gardens, went to the beach to listen to the sound of the waves, and kept silent when needed. He loved to be surrounded by the verdant atmosphere in the garden. He preferred to look at the trees and plants instead of looking at 'people who had no self-respect'. On such occasions, he would go to the garden of Krishnasamy Chettiar or to Villianur nearby.

Bharati's weariness would wear off after watching the birds, the pond, and the vegetation in the garden. Perhaps he might have felt that he was amidst living beings and aesthetic ideas. If he were mumbling swaras, then others beside him would be sure that he was composing a taal for his new lyrics. He would gaze at the trees and the pond. Then, thrusting his chest forward and lifting his head as much as he could, he would look at the sky. He would shout sa sa sa-sa sa ssa- sa sa sa breathlessly and tap his foot. If the tapping faltered, he would kick the ground. After a minute's silence he would yammer, "Speak thee white conch!"[1] Then a stanza from Thayumanavar, "Thou reared me as a wild elephant!"[2] He would again belt out 'Sa Re Ga-Ga-Gama'. It was a sight to behold the alternating states of excitement and weariness in Bharati. It could be said that he would sever all links with mankind. It was as if his ribcage broke upon the arrival of a new song. It is not untrue to state that Bharati's poems have in them traces of blood and the spirit of life.

The world cannot fathom the pain experienced by artists and eminent people every time they bring forth new ideas. The spirited ideas are differentiated from the logically minded ones, and emaciate those people during germination. It is true that such ideas are created at the cost of their health. One might ask why they do such things, but that is the cruel act of mother nature. It cannot be put to ridicule. Can one stop a mother from lactating soon after the birth of her child? Likewise great people always undergo labour pains when they create.

Ramakrishna Paramahamsa used to imagine himself in many roles to enact the various moods of bhakti. In order to undergo Radha's vicarious feelings of love toward Krishna, he dressed himself in a saree and behaved like a woman. He used to attach a tail behind him and sit atop a tree mumbling 'Rama' to feel Hanuman's devotion to Rama. This was not meant for fun or mere role playing. Babu Bipin Chandra Pal said that without possessing a poetic mind, the subtlety of creation cannot be understood. Poets, like children, have no malice.

Once, the two Tamil poets, Pugazhendi and Ottakoothar, had a brawl. Pugazhendi was a great poet. Ottakoothar's choice of words was exemplary. The Chola was fond of both of them. He requested them to recite their verses. Ottakoothar took the lead. Pugazhendi asked the king whether he should confront Ottakoothar or link with him. As per the King's wish, he linked his recitals with Ottakoothar.

Nature itself is a link. The living beings look separate, but they are all linked together. Take for instance the human body. The head and feet are joined by the body, though they perform entirely different functions, to our surprise.

> 'The crow and the sparrow are our clan
> The wide Sea and mountain are our cluster
> We see none but ourselves everywhere
> The more we see the merrier are we,'
> sang Bharati.

This is the kernel of advice given by poets. Their bounden duty is to explore the link that connects all beings with artistry.

The one who understands, "We see none but ourselves everywhere" is the poet. He has no enmity and hence no iota of weakness. Is there any objection for him to feel that, "The more we see the merrier are we"? Bharati would dance in merriment in Krishnasamy Chettiar's garden in Muthialpet. He would be ecstatic and sometimes behave crazily. When the energy of nature galvanized his spirit, how could he restrain himself?

Swaras in his voice; taal in his feet; the tapping of his hands; his entire body in *Abhinaya*. The bliss he enjoyed in his body and mind would be reflected in his eyes. Bharati would lie down in utter exhaustion on the floor after creating a poem, similar to the state of a woman who would relapse into sleep after delivery. It was as if his body, in which the dance of nature took place, needed rest in a natural pose; he would stretch his body with no pillow to support his head.

No one knew what could have caused his sudden awakening after a nap. To my eyes he resembled a grazing cow rushing to its bull calf, suddenly remembering it. The cow would pacify itself only after hearing the mooing of the calf or catching sight of it. It was as though he was afraid that the stimulation of nature in him had ebbed away. On these occasions, his visage would exude a charm totally devoid of conceit and arrogance. Just as the mind, after it became one with nature, would not shelter meanness, so also the face would not. I would never see his expressive face even if I were to live a thousand years.

If only a thousand Tamils had seen Bharati's face while he was creating a poem, then our nation would have salvaged itself. My heart aches since the great fortune I had enjoyed had not been similarly enjoyed by even a few hundred Tamils. I have already mentioned the wonderful poems written by a Tamil teacher Kanaga Subburathinam under the pseudonym Bharatidasan. He was a friend and disciple of Bharati. He gave some unique information about the garden.

"Storm whirls, sea roars
Awaken my dear,"

wrote Bharati of the storm that devastated Puducherry thirty years ago. It wreaked havoc on the whole of Tamil Nadu with storm waters flooding it. "Forest trees fell down and became timber", this became news all over the land. Puducherry is a city on the coast. The ruin the storm brought forth could not be measured. The beautiful trees of the Othiyansalai garden fell down. The telegraphic poles broke apart. Buildings were knocked down. The roofed buildings collapsed into tents. The whole city looked as if it had been bulldozed by ghosts.

Amidst all these calamities, the trees in Krishnasamy Chettiar's Muthialpet gardens stood in their place intact, said Bharatidasan. Both of us do not believe in miracles. Hence, to call their escape a miracle without adequate explanation is very difficult for me. It may be conveniently imagined that nature wished the garden untouched since it gave wisdom to Bharati. None but the poetic mind can divine the reason behind nature's game.

14

I AM NOT SURE WHETHER IN 1910 OR 1911 THE Tuticorin Sub Collector Ashe was shot dead.[1] Chennai State Police suspected a link between this murder and the Indian Nationalists residing in Puducherry. But there was no reason for the Chennai government to suspect Bharati for that. It was said that suspicion arose on the basis of the friendship between Aurobindo, who was accused in the Maniktala Bomb Case (he was acquitted later in that case) and Va.Ve.Su. Iyer who was a close pal of Barrister Savarkar. They were both living in Puducherry. We need not worry about all that. But the doubt had disastrous effects.

It should be said that after that incident the Madras Presidency Police encircled Puducherry. Hundreds of policemen from British India began to monitor activities around the houses of Bharati, Va.Ve.Su. Iyer, and Aurobindo. It all looked like a show of puppetry. If the patriots remained at home, the police would sit in a nearby place. If they went out, the police would follow them. Later on, the friends of the patriots were also put to trouble. The hot pursuit by the police also gave way to certain playful activities. They were caused not by the patriots, but by their friends. On seeing the police following them, they would enter the house by the front door and leave by the back door, making the police wait wearily for them at the entrance. Afraid of the black marks that they might get in their careers for letting the suspects give them the slip, they would shout pathetically. But Bharati, Iyer, and Aurobindo reproached their friends for such pranks. "What a mean act this is!" was Bharati's reproach.

Bharati and his friend had an argument over this.

Friend: It is unfair to reproach us about this. What harm did we cause to the police to justify their following us?

Bharati: The crime is you are friendly with us. Does that not have its benefits?

Friend: Would you say that if one were to use a book as a pillow, one would get knowledge out of it?

Bharati: We are not printed books. We are living books as per the government's estimate. What shall we do?

Friend: Good argument. It was said because their names rhymed, someone called Theethan was treated when Kathan was infected. The government might even pass an ordinance not to talk to clever people.

Bharati: Would the clever person keep quiet? He would try to strengthen his role. The government is afraid that we will educate those who approach us with patriotism. Is not the fear natural? If they are unafraid, then what is our worth? The government infuses regard about us into people which we may not get otherwise. I wish to thank the government for this through the Madras Assembly.

On hearing this, the friend, a Professor in a Puducherry college, laughed merrily. He was a great music lover, an expert in the French language, a raconteur of historical anecdotes, a bright and humorous speaker. His name was Subramania Iyer. Bharati was fond of chaffing with him during leisure. He too was fond of listening to Bharati's songs. At least once a day, he used to visit Bharati and enquire about his wellbeing. Bharati used to consult him whenever he had a doubt in the pronunciation of French words and their meanings.

Certain peculiar instances took place due to the commotion wrought by the police. Spies would go to see Bharati and Aurobindo in various guises.

One day, Bharati received this letter: 'Hey! The great bard! For the pleasure of seeing your resplendent visage and listening to your nectar-dripping lyrics, I arrived in Puducherry after a ticketless travel in the train. Now I am hiding in a place. I shall come to your house at seven in the night. Kindly dim the light of your lamp then. Your disciple, lover of letters, and well-wisher from Tirunelveli.'

The person arrived at seven in Bharati's house. But Bharati, instead of dimming the light, kept it bright and sang 'Maravar Pattu' aloud. In that song there is a line, "Should one live the wretched dog's life?" Bharati kept singing this line as the stranger entered listening to it. "Should one live the wretched dog's life? Shame. Should one live the wretched dog's life?" The stranger was well-built with a shaved head. He wore a saffron gown from head to foot like Vivekananda and had a clean bindi on his forehead.

Bharati stopped singing. The stranger bowed. "Ah, the householder should bow and the hermit should bless. Now a reversal has taken place! Dharma is ruined," Bharati ridiculed him. But the stranger did not smile and Bharati's suspicion was fortified. "Well. You have seen me. Please take your leave," said Bharati. But he was in no mood to leave. He spoke all the languages – Hindi, English, Tamil and Malayalam. Bharati was enraged.

"When can I see Aurobindo?" asked the man.

"Haven't you seen Iyer?" Bharati fumed. Only then did the stranger understand Bharati's anger, innuendo, and the import of his song. Before signing him off, Bharati said, "Ay, Arjun Sanyasi. Live a sensible and lofty life. Desist from desiring deplorable things."

Spies did not come only in *sanyasi* (monk) costumes. One day, a spy came as a diamond merchant. He fit into his role well. "Do you want precious stones?" he asked Bharati. Bharati's scorching look terrified him. "Hey! I have nine kinds of gems. Please recommend them to your government for a good price. Do you have the police diary?" The gem merchant got shocked. He became speechless. "My respects to the elders," he told Bharati and left.

Sometimes, to get to know Bharati's response to armed rebellion, turbaned and suit-attired Tamil 'pundits' would approach him. Most of them belonged to the secret police force. Bharati's look would pierce them like arrows. But all of them would understand Bharati's greatness. Sometimes Bharati would simply sing before them. They wore different outfits, but the innate love for the land would be with them lying at the bottom. Even those who did all this for a mere living would get back their natural love for the country on seeing Bharati. Bharati knew how to 'press' that nerve.

15

WHY WERE THE BRITISH INDIA POLICE ANGRY WITH Bharati and his compatriots? During the Boer war, the Boers laid siege to the forts in Kimberly with Lady Smith and English troops trapped inside. Similarly, the British police besieged Puducherry. Let no one think that I am using the word 'siege' loosely. With the exception of the East Coast of Puducherry, the police, both in uniform and in civil dress, were on bandobust duty on all sides. Apkari department officials also joined them. The suspects among those who came from Puducherry were formally frisked at the French border. Many were intimidated. Some were arrested and released later on the condition that they do not develop contact with the Puducherry patriots. Many Puducherry businessmen underwent this ordeal. Murugesan, a helper of Bharati, was kept in prison for a few months. After his release he looked like a scarecrow.

The police bandobust was operating without legal

sanction. How many do you think they were? The British India police had rented a bungalow exclusively for themselves. Abdul Kareem, the Deputy Superintendent, was at the helm of the force. The title Khan Bahadur has now been conferred on him and he lives comfortably with a pension. Kuruvappa Naidu and Rangasamy Iyengar were the two canny police Inspectors who served under him. They worked to encircle and trouble the patriots of Puducherry in astonishing ways. No less than two hundred Sub-Inspectors, Head Constables, and Constables worked under them. Head Constables and Constables were fed in the bungalow kitchen itself. All this elaborate surveillance was to monitor a mere ten patriots including Aurobindo, Bharati, and Va.Ve. Su. Iyer. When a member of the Madras Assembly raised a question to reveal the expenditure incurred by such activities, the government refused to reply.

The police force in Puducherry worked cleverly. Apart from those who followed the patriots, others contacted people according to their position or status. Constables contacted betel nut shop owners and pushcart drivers and warned them not to have any association with the patriots. Sub-Inspectors would meet higher officials and tell them about the treason of the patriots, and also warn them not to give any form of support to them.

The patriots of Puducherry were called by the locals as *Swadeshis* (natives against foreign rule). It was not easy to describe the sight of the British India police and French Puducherry police engaged in whispers everywhere – on roads, beaches, market places, and railway station.

Kuruvappa Naidu and Rangasamy Iyengar used to meet with Bharati. Rangasamy Iyengar frequented Bharati's house. It was not easy to tell if he intended to spy on Bharati or was drawn to Bharati`s poetry and conversation with him .

I spoke of spying. What was it about? The British India police suspected a slight connection between the Ashe murder and the Puducherry Swadeshis. One Arumugam Pillai of Tuticorin, upon turning as an approver in the Tirunelveli Conspiracy Case, made malicious statements about Puducherry Swadeshis.

Ottapidaram Madaswamy Pillai, another person said to have been involved in the case, escaped without getting caught by the police (Ottapidaram is a place near Tuticorin). Now, after thirty-three years, no one knows if he is still alive or dead. Police suspected that the Swadeshis had given him asylum in Puducherry. They tried by all means to find out his whereabouts. There was also an absurd rumour doing the rounds that the Puducherry Swadeshis had smuggled arms from France and other countries. This also made the police more vigilant. Under various guises as a *sanyasi*, poetry lover, lawyer, diamond merchant and patriot, the police had met with Bharati and other Swadeshis to extract information on this. Aurobindo was sequestered in his bungalow. But, Bharati and others did not confine themselves to one place. Also Bharati was guileless. He could not maintain a stern face to strangers. He treated even a traitor with utmost sympathy as one lost in direction.

If you were to know the rumours that were rife in Puducherry in those times, you would laugh. One of them was about a plan by the police to abduct the 'Swadeshis' from Puducherry on motor bikes. Bharati shook with laughter when this hoax of astronomical proportions was conveyed by a man who came running, bathed in perspiration. "The French Governor had issued an order to Swadeshis to leave Puducherry within the next twenty four hours. I saw the police were on their way to execute it," the speaker would rant like that. Bharati would enjoy it by saying, "Let all of us depart to Kailash as one pack. That is the wish of all Hindus."

Nandagopal Chettiar was a leader of one of the

political parties in Puducherry. He belonged to the Sembadava Chettiar caste, and traded in tapioca and groundnut. The mention of his name caused tremors in Puducherry, for he was a gang lord. Puducherry locals expressed their fear: "The Nandagopal *Bandu* (gang) comes. *Chako, Chako* (beware, beware)." He is no more.

A man, with fear in his eyes and a stammer, said that Nandagopal had a pact with the British police to hand the Swadeshis over to them in the next two to three days, using force.

Surprisingly, Nandagopal had chatted with Bharati and Srinivasachariar and left only a little while before. Police would give a dangerous twist to his meeting with them. They would also wrongly interpret the meeting as one designed by Nandagopal to extract information from them stealthily. Another rumour was about a plan to use a prostitute to seduce Bharati. He was the poet steeped in divine love with his poetry. Needless to mention the place from where it originated.

The last rumour made him writhe. "Imbeciles! What did they think of Bharati? Scumbags! Alas, the state of mind of our people has gone so low. What to do to uplift them?" He was deeply worried.

When the police encircled them in Puducherry, the Swadeshis were subjected to untold suffering, especially financially. There was no postal delivery – money order payments did not reach. Many difficulties arose due to the fearsome attitudes of the Puducherry public. Borrowing provisions from neighbours also became difficult.

Freedom for the nation, constituting a new world, and establishing unique ideals, were not small matters. Any amount of sacrifice seemed small to accomplish them. It is said the tears of the poor were equal to the sharpness of the sword. If there was no suffering for the esteemed, the poor would not shed any tears. It was imperative that great souls like Bharati, Aurobindo, and Gandhi suffered so that the people would have their conscience pricked.

When the Police heightened its guard on Bharati, there were three people who stood by him. One was Sundaresa Iyer, a Telugu man. He was a low-paid clerk in a firm that traded in groundnut. There was no limit to his help to Bharati, which he gave by pawning and selling his wife's jewels. He loved Bharati's poems dearly. Another man was Ponnu Murugesan Pillai. He lived two houses away from Bharati's house in Eswaran Dharmaraja Street. He was wealthy and well-built. An atheist. He was an expert in the French language. Bharati used to spend much of his time in his house.

Murugesan was very much interested in having critical arguments with Bharati. He would animatedly talk ill of Bharati's belief in God, and would not help Bharati with money. His eldest son, Raj Bahadur, was Bharati's disciple.

Murugesan Pillai's wife served Bharati very devotedly. She possessed stellar virtues and fed Bharati when he was hungry. I would not get enough satisfaction even if I wrote several chapters on her. More about her later.

16

MOST OF THE TIME, BHARATI WAS IN PONNU MURUGESAN Pillai's house. It was a big house with an upper floor. Bharati sometimes spent the night upstairs.

There was a good domestic helper called Murugan in that house. He had two brothers. His mother was a bold woman, and worked as a maid in Bharati's house. She was very thin with protruding teeth. She was deaf but understood signs of communication very well. Whether she received a salary from Bharati or not, she was dutiful, diligent, helpful, and took pride in her work. None could entangle her in arguments, for she always spoke the truth. Her name was Ammakannu. Bharatidasan told a story about her. It might have taken place much later. But it is better to tell it here where she has been mentioned.

Once, out of desperation, Bharati decided to leave Puducherry for British India. It could have been in 1917. He had reached as far as the railway station in a huff.

Who could have stopped him? Bharati's young wife Chellammal would not have dared to confront him. Neither would his friends, though they got wind of his departure. Ammakannu was not at home then. She might have stopped him by any means. She might have quarrelled with him, advised him, or prostrated herself before him to change his decision. When she learnt of this, she searched for him everywhere, but to no avail. Subburathinam (Bharatidasan) spotted Bharati at the railway station. Bharati was pacing up and down on the platform with choleric eyes. His face brightened when he saw Subburathinam. Is it good to maintain a tough face, to a third person not connected to the reason for his anger in any way?

Subburathinam pacified Bharati somehow and took him along with him. They took a ride in a pushcart. But Bharati was adamant that he did not want to go to his house in Dharmaraja Koil Street. The pushcart driver took a detour to arrive at Bharatidasan's house. Ammakannu was standing in the way with *sundal* and other snacks. She might have been told of Bharati's return by the young ones. Knowing that Bharati was hungry, she intercepted his journey and offered him food. Bharati was very happy. "It is *devamirth*," said Bharatidasan. That could have spurred the thought of *Devalok* (abode of Lords) in Bharati. He asked the pushcart driver, "Drive the *rath* [Chariot]!" This incident is unparalleled proof of how a word can give a man a rare imagination. *Devamirth* (ambrosia), *Devalok*, and *rath* are words that led to imaginary visuals. Without imagination, a man is not even a quarter of his self.

Ammakannu was a coolie. She was an old woman. You might wonder how did she develop a great devotion to Bharati when she had no formal education, and all she had was her goodness. But I don't. She was no ordinary woman. She was "Valiant! Image of Sakthi!". With her innate knowledge, she might have evaluated Bharati, who had the same natural qualities. She worked in Bharati's house untiringly. Her devotion was godly.

Ponnu Murugesan's sister had a daughter. She might have been ten or eleven years old. She had a wonderful voice. She used to spend her spare time at her uncle Murugesan Pillai's house. She had a great admiration for Bharati. That child never spoke too many words. She had ideal features: tolerant, ever-smiling, and composed. She willingly performed minor chores for Bharati because she liked his childlike attitude. He was a good playmate to children. Was there any state of mind which he could not imagine?

Ponnu Murugesan Pillai's wife was another example of womanhood. I do not remember her name. She is no more. The other two mentioned are still alive. Pillai's wife was a portly woman with a bindi, rounded like a little moon, adorning her forehead all the times that I saw her. She was about forty years old and active despite her heavy physique. She had two sons, Raja Bahadur and Kanagaraja. Raja Bahadur was a Bharati admirer, of whom Bharati would talk highly. When I was in Puducherry, Raja Bahadur had left for France for higher studies.

Raja Bahadur's mother was quiet and womanly in all respects. She did not speak to Bharati often. She might have thought of Bharati as her eldest son. She would attend to Bharati on time, right from placing water and tooth powder when he awoke to the subsequent arrangement of coffee, idli, and other such items with a mother's care. If such an oasis of little comforts had not been seen by the great people undergoing despair, they would have tightened the noose around their necks themselves.

Was Raj Bahadur's mother worried about India's independence? No. Was she related to Bharati? No. Did she understand his genius? Certainly not. Was Bharati the kind of person who did not give small troubles to others? No. Bharati did not know how to take care of himself in a daily routine. His clothes should be washed and kept clean. He should be approached at the right moment for providing food. Self-respect was of utmost importance to him. He would sing as if caught in a mood of frenzy in the day or night and would go on nonstop for two hours. Those who were in the street or inside the house might have lost sleep. But none complained about it to him.

He had a bad habit of spitting from wherever he was. It would fall on the floor of the house. Raj Bahadur's mother would never complain about that transgression. We never liked that habit of his, but we lacked the courage to point it out to him. Raj Bahadur's wife would wait for him to leave the room to clean it. No one dared to mention it, including the devoted Murugesan Pillai. Raj Bahadur's mother took care of him as would a woman steeped in the values of Hinduism. If such virtuous women were born in lakhs then our nation would be at par with any other nation in the world.

17

ONE MORNING AROUND SEVEN, AFTER I HAD HAD MY cup of coffee, a gentleman, short and plump, entered the house. He shouted, "Bharati", and then, after offering namaskar, embraced Bharati tightly. Bharati too was greatly moved. A few minutes went by. They were emotional enough but stopped short of shedding tears.

I had until then seen no one establish contact with Bharati through physical touch, and hence it was surprising. I had not known many of his friends from outside Puducherry, so I could not easily guess his identity. He spoke to Bharati. "I was afraid I mightn't see you. I was released two months ago. I searched for you everywhere. I was determined to meet you. How are you?"

Jail! Release! Determined to meet Bharati!

What did he mean? He also addressed Bharati informally. Who was he? From which jail was he released? What was he doing? I could not understand anything.

"Were your days in jail good? You don't seem to be fine. If your physique has undergone this suffering, then what can be said of the sufferings of others. You have food first. We will talk about other things later," said Bharati.

The man went to the backyard to brush his teeth.

"Hey! Do you know him?" Bharati asked me. I said no.

"He is Surendranath Arya. He is a good Telugu orator. One of my Chennai friends. He underwent six years of rigorous imprisonment." Presently Arya entered. After a modest breakfast he said, "Bharati! Do you know this? I have become a Christian. How could I describe the compassion shown to me by the Danish Mission priests when I was in and out of prison? I have become a Christian."

"I harboured a suspicion about that. What could you do? Hindu society in its present state gives opportunity to all of them. It is a society devoid of spirit." Bharati trembled.

"When I exited prison, none dared to talk to me. Wherever I went people were afraid of me. Only the priests gave pleasant countenance and helped me.

Other than clapping their hands together when they hear a sermon and cowering with fear inside their house, the Hindus do precious little. I didn't want to be in that gaggle at all. Are you unhappy about my conversion?" asked Surendranath Arya.

Bharati was heavily distressed. He said, "If every Hindu, and that too the one fortified in knowledge, intelligence, and patriotism, felt embittered by the frauds of Hindu society and converted to another religion, then what would await it? If instances of the woman killing herself for the misdeeds of her husband and the husband embracing *sanyas* become common, then what would happen to the state of the family? Henceforth you will have to obey the dictates of the priests. They may use your strong patriotism (here Bharati shed tears) for religious propaganda. It is wrong to advise you." While Bharati was talking, Arya shed tears copiously. I did not know what to do. If those beings fit enough to be described by Thayumanavar as 'wild elephants' started melting, then as a lad my reaction need not be told.

Arya spoke after a moment. "Bharati, I am leaving for America. Priests have come forward to help me. I think it is wise to accept it. Without honour one cannot live here. Before my departure for America, I wanted to see you. If I were a great poet like you, I need not have to go to a foreign country." Bharati's face betrayed no emotion. He spoke. "I do not want to change your decision. I agree that it is human nature to be thankful to those who helped. Otherwise the world would perish. But should thankfulness need to result in our utter transformation? Many misdeeds and blemishes may have crept into the ideology, rituals, and daily activities of the Hindus. We should strive to annihilate them. Instead, out of fright, taking asylum in other religions is unacceptable to me. There is truth in all religions.

"We may get angry with our Hindu people. But we should not think of ridiculing our tradition. From time to time, many spiritualists and pious human beings have appeared to sanctify the Hindu life. People like you are qualified to be among them. I am not very much in favour of your conversion as a Christian.

"Many of our youngsters who go to America and other countries for their studies return with their wives who belong to the white race. Under the present state in India, I think that shouldn't happen. If such a thing takes place fifty years hence it doesn't matter. Do not think I am advising you. I think I have the right to share the thoughts I believe in. You should never be weary in your mind. Go to America and do anything you like. But do not forget our country."

After Arya took leave of him Bharati was in dismay. "How can this land get salvation if it fails in its duty to safeguard those who come forward to work for its improvement? Arya is a good man. A brave man who wouldn't tire. If he gets weary and distraught, then, Parasakthi, only you can save this country." Bharati was talking to himself.

He was the same valiant Arya who tauntingly asked, "If you and the murrel fish both have moustaches, then what is the difference?" in a public meeting in Triplicane beach; the same Arya who got a Doctorate in Philosophy from America; the same Arya who came here to work for the Self Respect Movement. He was Bharati's long-time friend.

18

I HAD EARLIER SAID THAT SEVERAL HUNDRED POLICEMEN from India were camping in Puducherry. Puducherry locals sympathized with the suffering of Swadeshis like Aurobindo and Bharati. The police tried hard to expel the Swadeshis from Puducherry. First, they sought the assistance of the locals, who did not budge to their entreaties and threats.

The power and popularity of the Swadeshis grew day by day. 'Cercle Sportif', a youth corps founded in Odianchalai in Puducherry, was drawn to Aurobindo. Bharati enjoyed fame all over Puducherry. The police, unable to garner public support, sought the help of the Puducherry government. Top police officials met with the Puducherry Governor often. The gist of their conversations would somehow reach the Swadeshis.

Those who had no faith in the political order were called Anarchists and Nihilists in Europe. They were not given shelter there and anarchy was viewed as a dangerous crime. The police dubbed the Swadeshis as anarchists, and voiced ideas to that effect to the Governor. But the Governor wanted proof to act upon. What proof could they offer? The Governor refused to expel them.

It is said that some creatures could employ a thousand tricks. So the police went on for other tricks. Did not the heroes in ancient wars use divine weapons one after another? The police hit upon another ruse. Since the Swadeshis were foreigners to Puducherry, the police wanted the State government to deny them citizen rights. They wanted French India to enact the Foreigners Act in the Puducherry Assembly. If that act came into force then the Swadeshis would be driven out of Puducherry. The Governor agreed to that. Would any government obey the dictates of another government, it may be asked. But French India was in no position to go against the British.

France was in bad shape during the years 1911-1912. It thought the neighbouring country Germany, its sworn enemy under the rule of the Kaiser, was doing everything to discredit it. There was an old story that Kaiser destroyed Agadir Harbour in Morocco with his warship. The French government felt threatened by that and other similar acts. The External Affairs

Ministry thought that without the aid of England, France would not be able to withstand the hegemony of Germany. Hence the French government buried its hatred for England and began its overtures. The French administrators wanted it to be smooth sailing with the English. This led the French Governor to enact this law. But the Puducherry legislators did not dare to oust the Swadeshis, root and branch. The Foreigners Act had in it a clause allowing Swadeshis to continue living in Puducherry if they had resided there for a year and if they could obtain signatures from five Honorary Magistrates and register them with the Police.

It is not easy for anyone to understand now the efforts made by Swadeshis to include the section in the Act when the French government was under the influence of the British government. Who would the French Governor listen to, the Swadeshis, considered indigent, or the English? The Police did not mind the inclusion of the aforesaid section in the Act, since they were confident that they could stand in the way of the Swadeshis obtaining the signatures of five Honorary Magistrates.

What did the Kaiser achieve by thinking ill of the British Army? 'All is grist for the mill,' is a proverb that cannot be slighted.

Within days of the promulgation of the Act, Swadeshis (being foreigners) had to register with the police. But how would they find five Honorary Magistrates? At all times, the rich and the powerful support the government. The British police knew that when they agreed to the small correction in the Act. They thought the Swadeshis would be easily trapped by that. They had already contacted all the Honorary Magistrates and spent their time merrily.

The one-year stay in Puducherry mentioned in the Act was the last refuge for the Swadeshis to seek. They did not know who were the Honorary Magistrates. But they had to somehow find them. The Swadeshis grew despondent. Aurobindo, Iyer, Bharati, Srinivasachariar, and other elders discussed it at Aurobindo's bungalow. They could not find a way out. Needless to say, they were a little worried.

"Well. Let us talk about it tomorrow evening," said Bharati. It was nine at night. "Come tomorrow to my house at eight in the morning," Bharati asked me and then left for home. I was then staying at Aurobindo's bungalow.

The next morning, as soon as I reached his house, at eight on the dot, he asked, "Shall we leave?" Unlike last night, his face exuded confidence.

"Where do we go?" I asked him.

"Follow me without question," said Bharati. It was not clear to me why I should follow him without question. I was a bit angry. But it had no effect. I went with him silently. After walking some distance he patted me on my shoulder as encouragement. Like a Koel bird waiting for rain drops from the sky for sustenance, I found that very comforting. My anger left me without a trace. We reached the house of Sankara Chettiar. He was sitting on the swing inside the hall. He rose with folded hands saying, 'Swami.'

"Do we have to leave Puducherry when all of you are here? Are you aware of the new law?" asked Bharati. Chettiar had been in Chennai and he did not know of it. Bharati explained the Act. "This is simple," said Chettiar. Being a timid youth I was consoled by that.

"What shall we do?" asked Bharati.

"I can get five signatures. I am also an Honorary Magistrate," said Chettiar.

"Good. Can that be done today itself?" asked Bharati.

"It will be done in another two hours. Give me the documents for signing. I will meet you at your house in two hours," said Chettiar.

As though he suddenly got reminded, he asked Bharati, "Please sing a new song."

I was not certain if he improvised a song at that moment. He should have sung that new song two or three days ago.

Before three in the afternoon, Aurobindo, Iyer, Bharati, Srinivasachariar and all others had registered the signed documents with the French Police, who accepted them. We were relieved. The British India police who followed us were sorely disappointed. They forgot that God exists. They failed in every attempt.

After the failure of these small tricks, they went for a bigger plan. According to them, the English would swap some of the islands in the West Indies for the Indian territories under French occupation. It seemed the French government would agree to the proposal of the English ministers. Aurobindo wrote letters to important people like Laporte and Paul Blouson. Bharati's friend, Ponnu Murugesan Pillai, knew many influential French men living in Paris through correspondence. He also knew some well-known merchants.

The time was near to the French election. Swadeshis wanted to wait until the change took place. Bharati made Ponnusami and others write letters to France. I think there was a meeting held in Puducherry against territorial exchange. But I am not sure of my memory.

Laporte and Blouson tried hard. We were worried

that their efforts should not come to naught. The French Ministry underwent a change. Poincaré became the President (his name is often misspelt and mispronounced here in Tamil Nadu). Poincaré, when he assumed office, proclaimed categorically in the Chamber of Deputy Members of Parliament that "No land where the French flag flew would be traded. The soil where French blood was shed is sacrosanct for me and the French people. That too in Puducherry, where Dupleix's statue has been installed."

The despair of the Swadeshis was finally over. But the British India police were tenacious. Would they ever accept defeat and keep idle?

19

WE GOT THE SIGNATURES OF THE FIVE HONORARY Magistrates due to the sincere efforts of the humanitarian, Sankara Chettiar. All the Swadeshis in Puducherry were exempted from the *Estranger* (Foreigner) Act because of that. What a sight to behold! The police were dumbfounded. From the time the Act came up for discussion to its enactment in the Puducherry Assembly, the Swadeshis were in a state of anxiety. Even Aurobindo was visibly worried, not to mention the others. Va.Ve.Su. Iyer was severely distraught among the Swadeshis for no palpable reason.

But Bharati was singing like the Koel would in the spring season. There was no dearth of joy. Maybe he had confidence and courage that the 'adverse period' would not affect the Swadeshis. If someone had asked, he might have said that the Goddess Parasakthi would do the needful. Whatever that might be, those whom I thought strong-willed were sunken in spirit. But

Bharati, not viewing this as practical, was the most valiant who withstood the tough times.

The police, unable to accept the escape of the Swadeshis from their net, would go for another trick. The Swadeshis were uncertain of their next move. As Bharati said, Swadeshis were singing *khyal* in the meantime.[1]

But the Swadeshis underwent a different ordeal. Money Order remittances due to them were withheld at the Post Office. Bharati, who was thoughtless about money, suffered since he did not have even a small amount. Va.Ve.Su. Iyer was smart enough to have some means. Srinivasachariar too had money. So did Aurobindo. During such troubled times, patriots around the world used to help one another. But Bharati was offered no such help.

During those difficult times, there happened a miracle on one morning at Iyer's house. When the maidservant drew water from the well, something was caught in the pail. She informed Iyer about it. Iyer groped and found a sealed ink jar. The jar was slightly big. Iyer had a suspicion. He thought it was the enemies' pot. He wanted to break open and see what was inside. But he thought he should hand it over to the police untampered. He informed Aurobindo and Bharati. The jar was given to the police along with his statement.

The French police opened the seal and found notes. There was information about conspirators from Tamil Nadu having their headquarters in Puducherry. They also had descriptions about manufacturing bombs. There were also some nails and pins inside. No doubt that was a ploy to implicate the Swadeshis. The strategy was brilliant, but other details were idiotic. Neelakanta Brahmachari was the leader while Aurobindo and Bharati were ordinary members of the conspiracy committee, as per its details. The French police officer, who was twenty-five-years old and of similar rank to the British prosecutor, searched the residences of the Swadeshis. By designation, he was 'Juge d'iInstruction' and had the authority to confer with other judges and proclaim the verdict. He came to Aurobindo's bungalow. He saw on the desk a Greek book and a Latin book.

He asked Aurobindo, "Do you know Greek and Latin?"

"Yes," said Aurobindo.

The Officer left without further examination. He went to Bharati's house. There were many manuscripts.

"These are my poems," said Bharati.

"Do you write poems?" asked the examining officer.

"Yes," said Bharati. The search ended then and there.

The investigation at Va.Ve.Su. Iyer's house was severe as it went on for more than three hours. But the Police could recover nothing to satisfy them. Nevertheless, 'Swadeshis' were proceeded against. I was also caught in that.

They asked my name.

"V. Ramaswamy," I said.

"Va. Ra.?" They asked.

"Yes."

"Then you are not the Ramaswamy mentioned in the bit notice."

They released me at the beginning itself. The case went on against Iyer and Aurobindo for two weeks.

They exonerated them one after another. Finally, Iyer was also declared innocent. For some time after that the police lay quiet. The people ridiculed them. The Puducherry locals said that Dharma could not be defeated. After that incident, the government officials had not only reduced their suspicion of the 'Swadeshis' to a great extent, but also developed confidence in them.

The British India police, however, did not lower their guard. They assigned two policemen to watch every Swadeshi. We did not let go of this opportunity.

We preached to them about Swaraj. They would pretend to listen with a responsive look. The game was entertaining to both of us. Some policemen would try to delude us into believing that a few hooligans were out to kidnap us. After their third attempt to evict us was foiled, the British India police succeeded in blocking the payments from reaching the Swadeshis completely. Aurobindo too had no money after that. How to buy provisions for food?

I was then staying at Aurobindo Ashram. As two people at a time needed to cook, we took turns. One day there was nothing to cook. No money to buy vegetables. We approached Aurobindo. He wanted to know our stock.

We said, "Rice, dried chillies, gingelly oil, and salt."

"Boil the rice and fry the dried chillies," he said. We ground the dried chillies and mixed them with rice and salt. We ate that somehow, but Aurobindo, being a saint, ate it as he would the regular food.

Look at the fate of patriots and learned people under foreign rule! Can it be accepted as a common fate that Aurobindo, who had earned 1,000 rupees in the Princely State of Baroda, a polyglot and, according to Calcutta High Court Judges, 'a fine writer of English', was reduced to the condition of eating rice with dry chilli powder? But on the same day, Aurobindo was given two thousand rupees by someone. Was not that funny? This had also happened to Bharati several times. Once Bharati received a thousand rupees from Durban in South Africa.

It did not last for more than a week.

20

AMIDST ALL THIS COMMOTION, BHARATI SUFFERED A huge loss. Should it be said it was a loss to Tamil Nadu as well?

Bharati had almost completed the book *Chinna Sankaran Kathai*. If my memory serves right, it had twenty-nine chapters; a gem of a work.[1]

Do you want to know what it was about? It was not a novel. Nor was it his autobiography. It was full of humour. But it was not a funny story. Not a myth. It was neither a didactic work nor a play. Also it was not entirely a satire. Yet it had all of the above. It could be said that the book was an account of the Tamils' lives. It had no pathos. It was brimming with humour and ridicule.

Bharati always used to read his writings aloud before his friends. It was not to demonstrate his ability. He wanted to ensure that his writings were well understood by most Tamils. For the purpose of gauging the reaction of others, he used to read in front of them. While reading, he would study the faces of his listeners. If he detected weariness in their eyes, he would cease reading. He would replace an abstruse word with a more intelligible one. If the idea was hard, he would illustrate it with examples using modified language. Some of us heard him read *Chinna Sankaran Kathai*. It would trigger terrible laughter. We were afraid while listening that we would suffer displacement of our intestines due to hearty bouts of laughter. The sarcasm was not of the mundane variety. We found in it a sympathy for the state of our people.

How did the manuscript of *Chinna Sankaran Kathai* disappear? There was a domestic helper by the name Murugesan employed in Bharati's house. He absconded all of a sudden from Puducherry. The manuscript disappeared at about that time. Since it was logical to put two and two together, some of us dared to believe that Murugesan was the culprit. On hearing that, Bharati was incensed beyond limit. He spoke very well of Murugesan. He made us understand that if we suspected anyone who either belonged to our house or to our institution, then we would certainly be ruined.

"How could you call him guiltless? Why didn't he report to work for a week? Why did he run away from

Puducherry?" We queried him persistently. Bharati did not change his mind. He was silent.

After nearly forty days, Murugesan appeared. He was all skin and bone. He was beyond recognition. How did he become a scarecrow of a man? It was morning, and Bharati was in bed. We looked alternately at Murugesan with pity and suspicion. He was standing with his eyes full of tears. Bharati came there suddenly. Murugesan let out his grief and sobbed uncontrollably. Bharati cast a look at us and then with lightning speed, rushed forward to embrace him.

"Why do you cry? Is everything gone? Should a man cry?" He consoled him. We were flabbergasted. Bharati spoke to him with a smile.

"Hey, Murugesan! Where did you go? You had disappeared like Indrajit!"

Murugesan stopped crying and said, "A British policeman asked me to go with him to Villupuram. I liked the idea and boarded the train with him. When we arrived there I was told of my arrest. They took me to Chennai. They beat me cruelly.

'You are working for Bharati. Tell us what you know of him.'

'He writes poems that are understandable even to people like me with little education,' I said.

'Did we bring you to listen to this?' They tortured me for a month and then released me. They didn't give me money to buy the ticket to Puducherry. I borrowed money from a relative in Chennai to reach Puducherry."

Bharati was immensely sad upon hearing that. But we concluded that it was a figment of his imagination. Not that the police would not have done all that, but the way he narrated it aroused suspicion. Bharati allowed him to continue to work in his house. We were astounded by Bharati's open-mindedness. We could not appreciate it though. Bharati thought *Chinna Sankaran Kathai* had finally reached the police, but not through Murugesan. But we did not think in two ways like Bharati.

We grieved over the loss of the manuscript. We requested that Bharati write it again. He wrote six chapters and then he said his mind was not set on it. He never spoke about it. The six chapters were published in 'Gnana Banu' magazine run by Sri Subramania Siva. That Tamil Nadu had to be content with those six chapters was a matter for great sorrow. A few fools were murmuring that Bharati was a coward. They did not know of his nature. They used to speak highly of the way Va.Ve.Su. Iyer reached Puducherry from London incognito and asked if Bharati could have done that.

Surely Va.Ve.Su. Iyer performed a big feat. But should they speak ill of Bharati's courage?

Kodiyalam V. Rangasamy Iyengar was a great patriot. His family members were well-known, wealthy landlords in the Tiruchi District. Governors of Madras visiting Tiruchi would give their first audience to them. Rangasamy Iyengar, like the agarwood that burgeons out of cactus, was drawn towards nationalism from such origins. Iyengar was an ardent devotee of Aurobindo. He respected Va.Ve.Su. Iyer. He regarded Bharati as a patriot and not anything more. How could he have understood Bharati's great poetry in the years 1911-1912, when dimwits even now, in 1943, do not?

The English poet Lord Byron wrote the liberation poem, 'Isles of Greece', to arouse the Greeks from enslavement. Iyengar had made thousands of printed copies of it and circulated them freely. Yet he did not have the mind to appreciate Bharati's poetry. When thousands of Tamil patriots even now live with no love for the Tamil language, it was unwise to have looked for the same from Iyengar during those times.

But Bharati astounded Iyengar with an act. There was a hamlet called Nagai (not Nagapattinam) near Mannargudi in Thanjavur District, where Rangasamy Iyengar had a nice bungalow. Iyengar used to go and stay there often for several days. He narrated to me an incident that took place there.

"One day, at eleven in the morning, after eating food I was chatting with friends for an hour. A horse cart pulled up in front of the bungalow. The only man who was inside the cart stepped down without any luggage. He was bald, without a moustache, wore an unbuttoned shirt and a coat over that, a *Panchakachcham* (a dhoti with five folds) was around his waist, and a beautiful zari dhoti was on his shoulder. He came up the stairs speedily. At first I could not recognize him. I looked at him steadily. He was Bharati! I was surprised. He had shaved off his moustache. Others could not identify him either. Since I did not want them to know of him, I simply said, 'Please come.'

"At that time two warrants had been issued against him. There could hardly be a person in Puducherry who wouldn't recognize him. For the police too, identifying him wouldn't be a task. But then how could he reach Nagai? Va.Ve.Su. Iyer's journey from London in disguise did not seem to be difficult in comparison, since the police did not know him. But Bharati was a well-known person. Despite that, how did he manage to be invisible to them? I realized then that my estimate of him as a coward was utterly stupid. There is an adage in Tamil that says, 'Who knows what species of snakes would dwell in which anthill?' I realized very strongly that one should be very cautious before underestimating anybody.

"Bharati stayed with me in Nagai for a week. I introduced him to my friends. The whole week with him was full of joy and merriment. He didn't talk about politics. He sang and my friends were entranced by him."

Rangasamy Iyengar later told others and gave it publicity. It showed the extent of Bharati's courage. I have nothing more to explain.

Though considered to be a repository of respect and humility, Bharati would sometimes talk offensively. One such incident can be mentioned. One day we were enjoying the breeze sitting on the pier of Puducherry beach (the pier was one and a half furlongs in length and goods were unloaded there from the ships). Bharati was singing. A famous lawyer from Tiruchi, who was a friend of Va.Ve.Su. Iyer, was with us. After the song was over the lawyer enquired, 'How is Tilak?' He meant Lokmanya Tilak. Iyer's face turned crimson. He controlled his ire. But Bharati exploded. He addressed him in the singular.*

---

* Tilak was called respectfully by Tamils as 'Thilagar'. Throughout the book Va. Ra. mentions him as Thilagar. But here his name is given as it appears in English.

"Aren't you a Tamil? Are you an Englishman to call him 'Tilak?' Does your tongue refuse to call him Thilagar? He is our leader. Not your cowherd. You talk about him without regard, you idiot," Bharati spoke very nastily to him.

The lawyer's face grew pale. It was later known that the lawyer had actually no disrespect for Tilak. Tamil brahmins have the habit of referring to a person in the singular when he is not around. It is a bad habit among these people. The lawyer had unknowingly become used to that practice. That was all there was to it. The lawyer became sad. He sincerely apologized for his mistake. Bharati was greatly distressed.

"I feel sad and happy at the same time because you did it out of ignorance. I thought you had knowingly spoken ill of him. I spoke very harshly. Please forgive me."

Bharati was misunderstood in some places. But I wanted others to know the true greatness of Bharati that came out in those circumstances.

21

AT EIGHT ONE MORNING, I CASUALLY REACHED BHARATI'S house from Aurobindo Ashram. There was a small crowd gathered in the hall. I saw smoke, which I supposed came from the ritual fire. Some were chanting mantras. Bharati was seated on a chair. On another chair, a Harijan boy, Kanagalingam, was seated. Professor Subramania Iyer and several other important people were there.

I asked the Professor what was going on. He said the *poonool* (thread) ceremony was going on with the chanting of Gayatri mantra. I asked him again. "Is not the person seated, the Harijan boy Kanagalingam? Am I correct?"

"He is the same person. Bharati is imparting to him the Gayatri mantra (sacred chant)" the professor replied.

I was surprised. Only a few months ago Bharati asked me to remove the *poonool*. He had removed his own a long time ago. When that was the case, why did Bharati all of a sudden get this orthodox madness into his head, I thought. I sat silently. Bharati did not look at me at all.

After chanting the vedic mantra, he imparted another mantra to Kanagalingam. "From today you are a brahmin. Do not be afraid of anything or anybody. If someone asks you who made you to wear *poonool* tell him strongly, 'Bharati did it!' At any cost never remove the *poonool.*"

I looked around to see if anyone smirked after hearing this. But they all seemed to be in agreement with what Bharati said. After the function they left with *Tamboolam* (a traditional gift). Kanagalingam too departed. Bharati told someone, "You escort Kanagalingam to his house."

After everyone had left Bharati removed his *poonool.* "What man!" He laughed at me. "Your anointment is like calling Krishna a Brahmachari with all his frolicking with two wives and ten thousand female consorts," I said.

"As well-known brahmins, we do not need to wear a *poonool.* Since he is initiated into brahminhood, Kanagalingam needs it. I had it on me as mandated for the initiation ceremony. Now I do not need it." Bharati concluded his speech very well. Without giving further thought to it, Bharati proceeded to read out an article to Professor Sundaram. He had earlier held a discussion with him on the Gita.

The Gita discussion was entertaining. At that time in Chennai there was an English daily called 'Madras Standard'. Sri Ram Seshaiyar was its editor. He somehow kindled a discussion between Sri Sundara Raman and Bharati. Sri Sundara Raman's explication was on the traditional line. Bharati, being a modernist, conducted the argument according to his ways. Aurobindo was on his side. When Sri Sundara Raman took it forward unpleasantly, Bharati stopped forthwith. While the discussion was going on, Puducherry friends were surprised by one aspect of it. "Does Bharati know Sanskrit so well? Can he write in English with such grace and mastery?" They shook their heads with surprise. Many do not identify people around them as having extraordinary skills. That is the way of the world. When will it be liberated from such misapprehensions?

Bharati was fond of arguments, not for their own sake; he wanted to explain the truth. He had the same fondness for amusing others. At the end of Eswaran Dharmaraja Temple Street (near the seashore), there is a choultry. There, a puranic storytelling discourse took place. Bhagavathar, the narrator, was not efficient. The crowd did not enjoy the discourse. Bharati and I were there. The people began talking aloud. Bhagavathar had only one way to control the commotion. Every now and then he said, 'Gopika Jeevana Smarane' and the people responded by saying, 'Govinda, Govinda'.[1] Bharati did not keep quiet. Ponnu Murugesan Pillai had a servant called Govinda. He asked him to come over there.

"Govinda! You go and ask the crowd 'Why do all of you call me?'" Bharati prepared Govinda, and Govinda all too willingly participated in the fun. When Govinda asked the crowd, all but Bhagavathar and his accompanying artistes laughed merrily. Bhagavathar quickly brought his discourse to an end, and should it be said that his remuneration was also according to his performance?

A few might ask with anger and surprise: how did Bharati find time for all this when his mind was set on resurrecting the lives of Tamils? Only those who did not know how to enjoy humour would be angry with him. Those who knew Bharati would not be surprised at his abundant sense of humour. When Gandhi said, "Without humour I would have committed suicide a long time ago!" he was speaking for many like himself. After a hard struggle that ends in failure, a man would naturally wish to end his life. Only two things can save him from that. They are devotion to God and abundant humour, and they both supported Bharati.

Bharati was fond of playing cards and chess, but he was proficient in neither. Va.Ve.Su. Iyer was an expert in chess. He would knock off Bharati's pawns without consideration.

"Iyer, don't indulge in the killing game so hard. You may not have children," Bharati would implore him. For Iyer, pawns belonged to chess. For Bharati, pawns were his children.

In the card game, Bharati knew only 304. He did not even know that too well. He would have only me as his partner in the game. If he had got one or two jacks, he would be very happy and express it through his hand signals. He wanted to avenge his defeat by Iyer in chess through victory in the card game. I was amused by Bharati's childlike attitude given his extraordinary genius. Iyer and Srinivasachariar formed a team. Bharati and I were their opponents. Bharati would be greatly exhilarated if they were defeated.

"Iyer! This is the Waterloo that led to the fall of Napoleon. Henceforth you may have to go to St. Helena." (The island where Napoleon was imprisoned by the British government.)

Bharati wanted to swim in the sea. But he did not know how to swim. He would stand on the shore while Iyer and I swam. I had enough experience from swimming in the Cauvery river. I would go farther than Iyer into the sea. When we reached the shore Bharati would clap his hands with glee. "Iyer, your pride didn't click with my partner."

"What a child is Bharati!" I would smile then. Perhaps childlike behaviour is the hallmark of a genius. I had had the great fortune of a close association with the mathematical wizard, Sri Ramanujan. Even an inconsequential matter would be viewed with surprise by him. He would maintain a childlike face and exclaim, "Is that so?" At first I even thought he was being sarcastic. But he was a genius only in mathematics. In all other matters, he was like a child. I understood that later. Bharati too was like Ramanujan in some respects.

Bharati was very much fond of science. The pleasure he got from observing the sky through a telescope can hardly be described. He said the moon was closer to the earth. He was thrilled when the stars and planets, which looked like tiny specks, appeared magnified through a telescope. He would bring his wife and children to see the sky through a telescope.

Bharati noticed a slightly mentally deranged boy who was mostly silent. Bharati pitied him. He made a resolve to steer clear of his madness. "Madness is a mental illness. Let me take care of him." He meant to encourage us. He kept touching the boy often. He fed him with fruits after peeling them. He allowed him to sleep beside him at night. He affectionately addressed him as, "My dear! My Raja!" The boy received royal attention. We strongly believed that curing him would be achieving the impossible.

When Bharati was not around, we would jokingly imitate Bharati among ourselves. "Did you eat dear? My God. My copper. My dustbin. Devour the food!" Bharati's treatment went on dutifully for well over a month. In the end those of us who had ridiculed him were made to look stupid. The boy gradually recovered, and spoke and walked like a normal boy. Bharati was joyous. But he never took pride in his success. He spent more time in prayer in those days. The boy's parents shed tears of joy. They fell at Bharati's feet and thanked him. We exchanged foolish looks among ourselves.

Bharati kept himself away from the habit of taking opium, a habit he had come into contact with when he was with the Raja of Ettayapuram. During his stay in Puducherry for the first three or four years until 1911, the thought of opium never crossed his mind. Instead, he would lodge a whole nutmeg in a corner of his mouth and enjoy its secretions. Professor Subramania Iyer's cousin sister was living near Puducherry. She was a widow. She was fond of listening to Bharati's songs as sung by him. Once in six months, Bharati would go to Villianur in a pushcart. Once he took me with him.

One day, before taking a bath, he gave me a big nutmeg and asked me to chew and eat it. Hardly had I eaten half of it when I felt like levitating. My legs began to totter. Bharati took one for himself. The wretched stuff did not harm him. It was not clear why Bharati revived his opium addiction.

Was it because Tamils in large numbers did not appreciate his poems, or because of the absence of proper friends in Puducherry? I never knew that Bharati consumed opium until one day he asked his disciple in coded language, "Bring me the materials for the sacred fire!" I then learnt what it meant from the disciple. None of us dared to tell him, "You should give up that habit." But the opium addiction gradually ruined his health.

22

THE FRENCH GOVERNMENT HAD MADE IT DIFFICULT to publish journals run by Bharati and those that ran because of Bharati`s involvement in them. There was a good printing press owned by Saigon Chinnaiah. Chinnaiah had great love and regard for Bharati. But he was also afraid of the approach and attitude of the French government. So neither Bharati's book nor his journal could be printed in Chinnaiah's press.

Publishing was like a breath of life to Bharati. What would he do without oxygen? While he was being tormented, he came upon a request from A. Rangasamy Iyengar – now deceased – to write non-political songs and articles for 'Swadesamitran'.

There was no individual remuneration for his articles and songs. An assured sum of thirty rupees would reach him every month irrespective of what he wrote or even when he did not write anything for the journal. Bharati was not concerned about money.

He was happy that he had a journal to publish. It need not be foolishly asked why Rangasamy Iyengar gave only thirty rupees to Bharati. When the ownership of 'Swadesamitran' came into his possession, it was already running at a loss. That apart, that sum is now equivalent to a hundred rupees. Tamils should never forget Rangasamy Iyengar for remitting thirty rupees for Bharati's poems published every month, which went towards his subsistence. It is the bounden duty of Tamils to wholeheartedly appreciate Iyengar and his life force, C. R. Sreenivasan.

The family without difficulty could procure the victuals with the steady monthly income of thirty rupees. Could Thayumanavar's songs sung at Vedaranyam Pillai temple have seen the light of day without the patronage of his devotee, Arulaiar (Veer Shivaite)? Without him, Tamils would not have had the benefit of enjoying those songs. It might not be an exaggeration to say that the service of 'Swadesamitran' to Bharati was similar to that of Arulaiar.

Bharati wanted all men and women in Tamil Nadu to sing his songs. With the help of Professor Subramania Iyer's brother, Saminathan, he improved upon the taal and raga of his songs.

Bharati would have chosen a particular raga for his

song. If Saminathan suggested a different and suitable raga for it, Bharati would not hesitate to change it. If his close friends were also cognoscenti then Bharati would never spurn their suggestions. He would accept them without ado.

Bharati wanted to sing like an ace Carnatic singer and hence he learnt to sing *swaras* systematically. Whenever he chose to sing he vigorously practised it. He would begin to sing without bothering about others around him. He would continue singing well into the night. Neighbours listening to him would want him to go on without interruption. I had heard connoisseurs say that Bharati's voice was more nuanced and brighter than Maha Vaidyanatha Iyer and Pushpavanam.[1] Thukkada ragas like Behag and Sahana were disliked by Bharati.

Bharati would be chatting with friends on the *pyol* or its adjoining verandah at Professor Subramania Iyer's house. People like Elikunju Chettiar (Arumugam Chettiar earned that nickname because of his squeaky voice) who figure strikingly in Bharati's articles are real and alive. If an assembly was convened, then Bharati would be its chairman as well as its orator. Professor Subramania Iyer would intervene only to stimulate Bharati to take the discussion forward. Others would simply enjoy Bharati's talk. If Bharati had any doubt in the French language, he would consult Subramania Iyer and Murugesa Pillai. When Aurobindo first came to Puducherry, the Swadeshis used to meet there. Their discussions offered a supreme delight.

In his recent booklet, *Achamillai*, Rajaji had written that Bharati went through several stages in his life; from a patriot to a poet and in the end a seasoned spiritualist. He had concluded that the transformation was in accordance with the ethos of our land. Lokmanya Tilak anguished that the patriot who began his life as an extremist or a revolutionary would become a moderate when met with failure, or he would join the Ramakrishna Mission and become involved in flood and famine relief work. Rajaji's remarks (of course I agree that they were made with good intentions) on Bharati affirm the observations of Lokmanya Tilak. Bharati did not like this transformation. He had liked Aurobindo since he worked tirelessly to attain independence for India. But when he learnt Aurobindo was drifting away from political struggle, he gradually reduced his contact with him.

Bharati was not a self-introspecting performer. If he were to ask for a boon to live forever, he would do so only to live on earth with pride. He fiercely opposed slothful men who prayed to attain heaven faster. We should regard his song 'If food is denied to an individual then we should destroy the world,' as his final statement. There is no inane Vedanta in this poem. Bharati was no mean person when he proclaimed, "All are kings of this land". It is regrettable that quite meaninglessly Bharati was grouped with ineffectual Vedantists.

Bharati was a consummate patriot. He had an inordinate faith in the arts. "If poesy and art gushed forth, the blind, fallen in ignorance, would emerge with sight." Is there any senseless Vedanta in those telling lines of the poet? Bharati loathed the basic Maya concept of Vedanta. "The wife stands like a golden statue. She melted in cries over our sorrows. She glowed with joy over our happiness. She brought up our children. Was she an illusion?" Bharati asked in anguish. To call Bharati a Vedantist is a big blunder. Besides, the contention of a few that the final growth of a person as a Vedantist is in consonance with the spirit of the land has led to perversities.

It may be that a person who encounters failure after failure in his efforts deteriorates as a Vedantist. The affliction born out of not getting the desired thing cannot be termed as 'the goal of the effort.' It is like the story of the fox that called the grapes sour when it could not have them. The ultimate goal lies in enjoying the fruit fully. Our platform speakers wrongly say that the base of our civilization is destitution; in other words simplicity and despair. And such civilization is unequalled in the world. When the white man brought the civilization of wealth and comfortable living to our country, our ancient simplicity and despair left us without any trace. That shows our people did not accept despair wholeheartedly, since it was imposed on them for generations. Was it not made clear that when the opportunity came, our people were ready to shun it?

For centuries, due to the influence of Maya philosophy, our people have failed to strike a compromise between material well-being and spiritual aloofness, and as a result they are unable to identify their goals for a life of freedom. This is our history.

The long past of slavish Hinduism is a grim reminder that people should not grow into obsolete Vedantists due to despondency. To cite the example of Vidhur, who spoke about Dhritrashtra: "Brother! If the ear that listens is also lost?"

Bharati was not a sham Vedantist. He was a great poet. An artist without parallel. A true spirit who was born to rule and enjoy the world. Therefore, people like Rajaji should not shut Bharati in a tiny Vedanta casket through their deceitful ploys.

23

BHARATI (ASIDE FROM POLITICAL DISTURBANCES) LED a wholesome life in Puducherry for ten years. He would visit anyone's house to attend any function, like a marriage, if invited. He would not enquire about their caste. He had addressed meetings on social problems in several places in Puducherry. It could easily be said that he had won the wholehearted admiration of the people of Puducherry in those ten years.

Pushcart drivers greatly liked him. He would readily give what they asked. The angavastram that Bharati might have got from Duraisamy Iyer of Chennai or from somebody else would become the property of a pushcart driver the moment he cast his eyes on it. "He wants to wear the zari dhoti. Where will he get the money from? Who will buy it for him?" That was the explanation Bharati would give for his generous act.

Of those who helped Bharati, a special mention must be made of Kuvalai Kannan and Sundaresa Iyer.

Kuvalai Kannan was faithful to him like a hound to its master. He rendered a lot of manual help to Bharati. If anyone talked ill of Bharati then he would surely have slapped him on the cheek. Sundaresa Iyer was working as a clerk for the groundnut merchant Kuppusamy Iyer. It was Sundaresa Iyer who helped Bharati by giving him money dutifully under straitened circumstances. I knew that he gave the money to Bharati by pawning and selling his wife's jewellery. He was that devoted to Bharati.

I had already said that Muthialpet Krishnasamy Chettiar, who was fondly nicknamed Vellachchu Chettiar by Bharati, was Bharati's devotee and friend and would never visit Bharati without offering him help. Every time he visited he would give Bharati no less than ten rupees. He visited him two or three times in a month.

The family of Ponnu Murugesan Pillai regarded Bharati as a member of their household. The devotion and love shown by the housemaid Ammakannu to Bharati cannot be described by me. She was unique and bravehearted.

Bharati was of the opinion that the First World War would bring many benefits to India. In 1918, he knew that his dream had been meaningless. After that he did not like to live in Puducherry. He decided to return to British India and wrote to A. Rangasamy Iyengar about that. Iyengar suggested that it was the ideal time for his return. As soon as Bharati crossed the boundary of French-occupied Puducherry, he was arrested by the British India Police and held in the Cuddalore Sub Jail.

A. Rangasamy Iyengar, after hearing of Bharati's arrest, met with the Madras Police Inspector General and presented him with the facts about Bharati. The Police Inspector demanded an assurance from Bharati that he would not participate in active politics. But Iyengar pleaded that to demand an undertaking like that from Bharati would demean his finer sensibilities. He also informed him of Bharati's worsening health. With diplomatic tact Iyengar worked on a compromise agreement that did not give Bharati up but was acceptable to the police. He arranged for Bharati's release and assured him of a job in 'Swadesamitran' at all times.

Bharati stayed for some time in Kadayam, in the Tirunelveli District, before he returned to Chennai. Rangasamy Iyengar renewed his offer to Bharati in 'Swadesamitran', irrespective of whether he contributed to it or not. Bharati resided on a street next to Parthasarathy Temple in Triplicane. The story of his efforts to be on fraternal terms with the temple elephant was fantastic. Whenever Bharati visited the temple he brought with him coconut and fruits not as offerings to God, but to the elephant kept tied at the entrance of the temple. He gave it the offerings, wanting the fraternal love of the elephant in return. He also sometimes fondled its trunk with his hands.

Bharati thought the relationship was improving. But one day, when he offered the fruits to his 'brother' elephant, it turned wild and dragged him inside the fence where it was bound. The bystanders were alarmed that the elephant might trample him under its feet as Bharati lay motionless inside the fence. Kuvalai Kannan, after somehow learning of the mishap, ran to the place as if he flew there. He jumped the iron fence, lifted him, and delivered him over to those standing on the other side. Bravo, Kuvalai Kannan! Who else but Kuvalai Kannan, who was dearest to Bharati, could have done that? The elephant was in musth, but would that have bothered Kuvalai Kannan in the least?

Bharati was saved. Kuvalai Kannan emerged from behind the fence. If someone were to photograph a hero who was fearless about his own safety, then Kuvalai Kannan should have been photographed as he showed up there. Bharati, who sang:

'The crow and the sparrow our clan
The wide sea and mountain are our cluster,'

did not live long after this episode of seeking brotherhood with the elephant. He had suffered contusions all over his body due to the elephant's misbehaviour. They caused him unbearable pain. The pain subsided later, but he died three months after that incident.

'IF TOO HEAVY A BURDEN RESTS
ON A STONE PILLAR
IT MIGHT RATHER CRUMBLE
BUT NEVER BEND'[1]

The elephant which had adopted a brotherly attitude to Bharati played a dirty trick on him in the end. Its act weighed as a heavy burden on Bharati's heart. Rather than bend and adjust in his feelings, which was against his nature, his heart could have broken without others knowing. Bharati died on 11 September 1921.*

I was told, by his devotee and a great patriot, that the funeral expenses of one of the great poets of the

* Bharati died at 1am on 12 September 1921 as per Christian Calendar. The author has mentioned the date according to the Indian system, where the day starts only at sunrise.

world could not be met by his family but only with the help of his devoted friends. I am submitting the fact as it was conveyed to me. I hope Tamils would introspect in this regard.

Before I conclude, I wish to record one or two incidents. Bharati often used to address meetings in Triplicane beach after his return from Puducherry. Hundreds of youngsters would gather and wait for a long time to listen to his speech. In one of those meetings, Sri Sathiyamurthy and another (whose name I have forgotten) had spoken earlier. It was convened for Bharati's speech, but Sathiyamurthy cheekily announced to the crowd, "Bharati, to whom you usually listen, will address you tomorrow. The meeting is over today." He left immediately, but the crowd stayed put. Bharati got up and darted his sallies clothed in well-chosen words at Sri Sathiyamurthy.

Bharati harangued the crowd amidst torrents of applause. When the meeting ended it was eleven at night. In that meeting, he sang the immortal song 'Hail! Bharat Community!' for the first time. Could there be any other reason for the crowd to stay until eleven at night? It was a surprise that Sri Sathiyamurthy, who praised Bharati greatly in later years, did not understand him properly in those times. If anybody other than

Sathiyamurthy had behaved in such a manner, the event might not have caught our attention. Also, mention of the event was made to record it as the occasion when the song '*Bharata Samudhayam Vazhgave!*' (Hail! Bharat Community!) was sung for the first time.

There was another incident that was alternately joyous and sorrowful. Bharati had sung five songs on Mahatma Gandhi. Every word of those songs could fetch lakhs if monetized. But you might have been surprised as to why we had not heard of any meeting that took place between them? Bharati and Mahatma met and talked. In just one meeting they understood each other very well.

Gandhi came to Chennai in February 1919. Many Indian leaders wanted Gandhi to lead the protest against the repressive Rowlatt Act.[2]

Rajaji was then living at No.2 Cathedral Road. Gandhi stayed there for four or five days. One afternoon, at two o'clock, Gandhi was as usual sitting, leaning on a bolster. Mahadev Desai was taking down his dictation. Late Salem barrister Adi Narayana Chettiar was making juice out of *kudagu* (Coorg) oranges for the Mahatma. Sathiyamurthy and others were leaning against the wall. On the opposite wall Rajaji and a few others were leaning. I stood outside as a guard, with strict instructions not to let anyone inside. Please don't make fun of my guarding. While conversation was going on inside the room, Bharati briskly entered, addressing me, 'Hey! How are you!' I dropped my vigil and followed him inside. Bharati bowed to Gandhi and sat beside him on the bed. He began to talk:

Bharati: Mr Gandhi! At 5.30 this evening I am addressing a meeting at Triplicane beach. Can you chair that meeting?

Gandhi: Mahadev bhai! What is our program this evening?

Mahadev: At 5pm this evening, we have an appointment elsewhere.

Gandhi: In that case it may not be possible today. Could you postpone the meeting to tomorrow?

Bharati: Not possible. I am leaving, Mr. Gandhi. I bless the movement you are going to start.

Bharati left. I too followed him to the entrance. After Bharati's exit Gandhi asked, 'Who is he?' Rangasamy Iyengar might have thought that he should not speak highly of Bharati, whom he was patronizing. So he was silent. Sathiyamurthy was also silent since he might have angrily viewed Bharati's occupying a seat on Gandhi's bed as a disrespectful act.

Rajaji said, "He is the poet of our Tamil Nadu." Gandhi listened and said, "He should be given good care. Is no one to do that in Tamil Nadu?" Everyone was silent.

Consider this event. Some may think that Bharati should not have conducted himself like that. Should Bharati have remained a supplicant before them in the room which had no chair to sit on? Shouldn't people like Rajaji have introduced Bharati to Gandhi properly? Gandhi made the correct estimate of their silence and of Bharati, as he entered casually. Otherwise, without consulting Mahadev of their engagements, Gandhi would have said, "I am attending to an important work. It would be good if I am left undisturbed." Bharati would have understood the implication and left. It is said that a snake identifies the trail of another snake. Was it not possible for Gandhi, the wise man, to identify Bharati by his wise visage? Besides when Bharati said, "I bless your movement," would it not have been possible for Gandhi to conclude that he was an important person?

24

GONE WERE THE DAYS WHEN PEOPLE SAID THAT Bharati's poems had a certain standard. They have now risen in stature enough to doubt if they have their equals anywhere in our country or in any other country. In a few years' time, it is certain to be felt that their match cannot be found anywhere.

Everywhere in the world, poets are artists. As artists they draw beauty, ugliness, and injustice with their words. It is rightly said that they were witnesses, but not participants. A 'poetic mind' could not be seen to a great degree in them.

What is, then, the 'poetic mind'?

'Poetic mind' is that which is inseparable from all beings of creation and their motions. The artist can see himself as distinct from his own creations. But the poet can never be like that.

If a poet writes a poem about a storm, then he is inseparable from the storm. He becomes love itself when he writes about love. When he attacks injustice his mind rises in anger. If the poet ridicules somebody or something then it will appear that he is ridiculing himself. His mind is one with everything. He speaks for others and cannot remain a witness. They alone stand qualified as great poets of the world. 'The great poet of the world' is the qualification given to them. Bharati would soon get that qualification since he had the poetic mind that could not be seen anywhere else. To express the poetic mind, scholars have found some theories called 'Navarasas'. The way in which the poetic mind conducts itself in its path, with its quality and speed, is distinguished as rasa or beauty.

Bharati's poetic mind could be sensed from its outpouring of the Navarasas. It was not enough for him to stay quiet after delineating the characteristic trait of the rasa embedded in it. He had the artistry to present it in its fullness with vigour and beauty. The poet who handles the Navarasas with ease can effortlessly attain greatness without anyone's help or recommendation.

Then why has he still not received international recognition, it may be asked. There is a saying that the ghost haunting the pipal tree also possessed the God Pillaiyar sitting underneath it. A similar threat is faced by Bharati. Bharati's inability to attain world renown owes to the incompetent, aimless, and lowly existence of the present day Tamils. There is also another reason. The world is presently applauding the brute and not the poet. It cannot see the difference between the poem and the sword. We should develop our pride and courage over the fact that Bharati will be in a principal position among poets to attain glory in the next several hundred years.

I shall give examples of the flowering of his poetic mind here.

"The crow and sparrow our clan
The wide sea and mountain are our cluster"

Don't you see how surprisingly he maintains love between live and inanimate objects?

"Difficulty will not make us fear
Poverty will not give us a scare."

The mounting of anger in Bharati can be seen here.

"Our mother will nourish and bless the good ruler
Of the wicked she will devour and dance."

Has anyone described a historical fact so beautifully as this?

"If a painting is bought by selling the eyes
Will that not invite ridicule!"

What a beautiful and powerful description!

"With slavery abolished in our land
Men and women are to live as equals."

Bharati's firm beliefs never failed.

"Reports of forests turned into firewood
By the torrential windstorm."

What an analogy for the tyrants who bit the dust! 'Reports of forests turned into firewood!' Only Bharati could have written like that.

"If no food is provided for a single man
The whole world should perish then."

Have you ever seen or heard of a poet with so much love and passion (except Bharati)? That everyone is the lord of the land is the unique credo of Bharati.

"On themselves who heap unease
Will find in God eternal peace."

What an effortless alliterative style without endangering sense!

"Let us not believe the world is sorrow
All we yearn is joy"

Look at the wondrous way Bharati demolishes the fake ideology that the 'world is an illusion.'

"We stunned the God of death
Who covertly enters to destroy life!"

This is surely an item for a triumphant drumbeat. There is no doubt of that.

"The scorpion in the pot with its teeth it bit,
at home a wife got possessed by a ghost,
twelfth-day ceremony to commemorate the death of
a granny"

The lame excuses of the dodging servants were described in a wondrously humorous way.

"Kannama my little angel
Thou art the granary of wealth"
"Kannama thou art nectar of fruit
Thou art the talking image in gold."

Regardless of one's own years, none can draw the picture of a child like this. Child, a talking image in gold!

"He will make me cry for the
Flower he has brought
Close your eyes. I will adorn you
When my eyes are shut he will
Adorn my friend"

Can the lover's prank be better described than this?

"For me thou art love
For thou I am the magnet
For me thou art wisdom
For thou I am the talent"

Bharati has gifted us a world of unparalleled imagination where lovers are in union.

In *Kuyil Pattu* (Kuyil song) there is joyous humour

from beginning to end. It is hard for me either to choose or reject any of its contents. Bharati is atop a humorous summit where humour is the least disturbing to others.

In *Panchali Sabatham* (Panchali's Vow), heroic qualities can be seen penetrating all throughout. Bharati called it a 'translation', with humility. Those who have read it asked me if its majesty, heroism, brilliance, word power, and the depth of its content could be found in the *Bharat* (Mahabharat) written by Vyas. How can we call Panchali's Vow a secondary version, if it towers above the primary version of Vyas?

If one were to read *Oozhi Koothu* (The Dance of Doomsday), then they would get a heightened feeling. I asked a Tamil, well versed in English Literature, "Have you read anything similar to 'Oozhi Koothu' in English?" He said, "No", and added that it was a poem with full of surprises. "A real dance of doom and no doubt about it." He heaved a sigh. It is not easy to assign a suitable place to Bharati among the great poets of the world since he uniquely portrayed the Navarasas in his poetry. Separate research has to be done on this. Let us see who is going to undertake it.

25

BHARATI DIED ON 11 SEPTEMBER. TAMILS EVERY YEAR celebrate that day with great interest. It is one of those rightful things to be done by Tamils with pride. But it is doubtful if Tamils properly understand the dignity of the Tamil language and the greatness of Bharati.

No great man working in his field is respected during his lifetime. Did they respect the great bard Shakespeare while he was alive? Simpletons who called him 'a deer poacher' were in great number in his days. Today, the whole world is immersed in joy when his name is spoken. Great people are largely the butt of ridicule during their lives (Gandhi is an exception to this). Hence, there is no use in lamenting over the fact that Bharati was not respected by Tamils. The prophets with their power find out external truths suitable to all times and occasions that others do not realize. The glutton has his eyes on food; the thief on thievery; the philanderer on women; the trickster on the gullible.

With such mean people around in large numbers, the wise sayings of great people are not given respectful attention.

Bharati too was 'respected' for some time in a similar manner. Pundits called him a poet who knew no grammar without any rhyme or reason. Many called him a poet of mere nationalistic poems. Some angrily called him a comrade of women's liberation. I have also heard some badmouth him as a 'ganja poet'. 'Wasn't he that Bharati who bought a basket of greens, not knowing to buy anything else in the market?' That was how some maligned him. But these allegations were proof that anything could be said without base and forethought, but not anything valid as criticism on Bharati.

Salvation for the human race can be had only through art and poetry. The all-pervading joy is in poetry. Philosophy may be full of logic. Physics may have an abundance of physical facts. People may experience feelings of devotion in religion. In love we may get tenderness, music, and consideration in great degrees. Art may be brimming with beauty and joy. But I worship poetry, which encompasses all of the above, as God. I say it aloud that Subramania Bharati sang poems that are unrivalled. He grows in stature always, and is seen as a progressive poet by the world. Bharati is the sun for all the devotees who look skyward, hands clasped with devotion. What if pundits roar? What if lay people are dormant? What if English-educated youngsters blabber out of prejudice? What if Bharati died prematurely after undergoing turmoil?

"He left nothing untouched. He touched nothing that he did not adorn." said Dr. Johnson of the great writer Goldsmith.[1] Can this not also be said of Bharati, with even more emphasis? From child to grandmother, lover to womaniser, monkey to koel, disbeliever to believer, scoundrel to poet, moron to Gandhi, angel to monster, scamp to Kamban – who has not and what has not been touched and embellished by Bharati? Bharati's poetry cannot be fathomed, nor can its boundaries be seen. Bharati would be praised both by the hedonist and the ascetic. As the drops that fall from above join together and reach the sea, human beings with varied characteristics reach the waveless mind, the great poet. Therefore the great poet belongs to all. He is common to all countries. Not just because people like Shakespeare wrote in English and became great poets. They became great poets because they captivated the minds of all.

Do you want humour in Bharati's poems? Yes, it is there. Do you want miracles? Yes, they are in abundance.

Do you need anger? It is there in overwhelming measure. Consolation? It is found in numerous pages. Spiritual freedom? It is in many writings. Why keep on extending? What is it that is not available in them?

I am afraid of Bharati, since every time I read his works I find new meanings and beauty in them. Bharati's wide platform accommodates all of us. How unique are Bharati's poems! I have said this a long time ago. Rajaji, during Bharati's celebration week in 1943, said, "In the past three hundred years there was no poet equal to Bharati in regional languages like Telugu, Gujarati, and Marathi. Bharati's avatar in Tamil Nadu is a fortune bestowed on Tamils." The incomparable Tamil savant Thiru.Vi. Kalyanasundara Mudaliyar said, "This is Bharati's era. Bharati created a superior revolution in the minds and lives of Tamils. His poetry is superior to the poetry of Tagore. He is a great poet of the world."

It took twenty years for these worthies to call Bharati a great poet of the world. At least they have come forward now to say this without inhibitions, and this is a matter for consolation. I do not want to dissect Bharati's poetry section-wise or piecemeal for study. It would be wise if it is done separately as a book. This book is written with the exclusive intention of introducing him through certain descriptions.

One thing the Tamils should take note of: nowadays several stories are translated into Tamil from Bengali and Hindi. What is the reason? Does it mean we lack in the number of writers in Tamil? Many writers who have begun to write are influenced by Bharati. But still Tamil has not been given its due recognition. It can be said firmly that caste pride and unwanted jealousies are the major causes. Bharati had said very clearly that Tamils can be transformed only through Tamil literature. That was why he laid the dictum, "Go across in all eight directions" before Tamils. We should strive to carry out the order by bringing all the riches to Tamil. Bharati is Tamil. If one were to pay devotion to Bharati, then they should do service to Tamil and the nation.

This is my request.

26

AS FAR AS TAMIL NADU WAS CONCERNED, THE PERIOD Bharati was born in was peculiar. The city was not crowded.

The village was not ruined. People were lamenting without knowledge that the cycle of famine and rain was the result of God's *leela* (divine play). Coffee was unknown then. People were tossing their *anna* (quarter) coins playfully. It was a time when people got happiness by watching Therukoothu[1] and the car festival. Fortune telling Valluvars, while predicting the fate of the well-educated, set the upper limit as Tahsildar, as they had no knowledge of higher positions beyond that. People mentioned the post of High Court Barrister in hushed whispers as though they were mentioning a celestial being. Diamonds did not adorn the hands, ears, or chests. Cotton saris, not silk saris, was what many had known.

It was a period when people derived education by

intently listening to spiritual discourses. Bharatanatyam was patronized only by the unlettered. Englishmen were praised for all the efficiency, save for the one to resurrect the dead. People used to wonder if there could be any calamity during the reign of Queen Victoria. It was not possible to see a cash roll of a thousand rupees in the village. Currency was scarce. Earning for subsistence was the major concern of the people. Those who travelled in chariots pulled by two horses were considered affluent.

What do you think of the condition of Tamils in those times? Thayumanavar had sung of the "routine habit of eating to satisfy hunger and sleeping." Tamils led a life similar to that. Did Tamils worry about art? Education? Gold? Politics? Poetry? Did they ever think about the Tamil language developing wrinkles like skin? Did they worry about handicrafts? "When the English, as the representatives of the Almighty, are governing with justice, what is the need to bother?" was what they prattled.

Would it be possible to escape them without injury if someone were to tell them that the English's safeguarding of justice was aimed at filling their coffers? "Do they interfere with our religion? Do they want to marry our women? Do they harm our orthodoxy? After all, they only take some money from us. So what if they do that? Will not the honey-gatherer lick the back of his palm flowing with honey?" That was how defensively most of our people spoke of the English rulers. Mostly, everyone wanted to be like the Englishmen. As preparation for this, they showed enormous interest in learning English. The English brought in their luxurious items from England when India was in dire poverty. Naturally the Tamils wanted to enjoy them. But they forgot that they lacked the means to buy them. They did not bother about that. They deceived themselves into believing that everything would take place according to fate, and that they had no role to play for themselves.

The ultimate effect was that responsibility and initiative took leave of the Tamils. They were reduced to a state of recklessness. 'I stepped on the thorn' should be the proper form of expression. But the Tamil would say, 'The thorn pierced into me', blaming the thorn and bearing no responsibility, even to a small extent. He rejoiced over his irresponsible, lazy life. Would the lazy man do anything? He would not sway even his little finger. He had no faith in earning through hard labour. Instead, as an alternative, to it he believed in luck.

The illusion called luck had other names. Time

was one. The grace of God, the Goddess Lakshmi's benevolence, and the mercy of God were a few others. He would thus fall into the pit of foolhardiness. Besides, there was the belief that one could advance in life only through the backing of others! The concept of fate also encircled them. What was the need to overpower Tamils when they were in such subservient conditions? They were rolling like balls, and the foreigners kicked the balls in the direction they desired.

Tamils fell prey to the false propaganda that they could call nothing their own. The propaganda too was done through English and other languages. They neglected the Tamil language. They raised obscene questions, like whether Tamil would feed their mouths and buy the clothes to wear around their waists. They forgot to respect their own possessions. They chose to argue that a government job would lead to *moksha* (eternal deliverance) rather than to *mukti* (spiritual liberation). Self-confidence, thirst for freedom, and self-respect ceased to be factors for Tamils. Subservience had reached its summit. Helplessness and sighs of relief were all that we had in return. It was true that, like an oasis in the desert, pride was welling in some Tamils. But they were dumb without activity.

Vivekananda did not believe in God when he was

young. He approached Ramakrishna Paramahamsa with that state of mind. He asked Paramahamsa if God existed. The answer was "Yes."

"Can you show him to me?" asked Vivekananda.

"Happily I will show you."

Vivekananda's vision underwent a fundamental change. Had Paramahamsa been a mere sadhu, he would not have effected even a small change in Vivekananda. Sadhus with mere Tamil pride could not enlighten the Tamils about a superior life. Others ridiculed them for indulging in twaddle. Could it be possible for sadhus to bring about a change in Tamils? The Vedantist, after the ruin caused by floods, droughts, and the displacement of people, believing only in the surrender at the feet of God for his deliverance, and the mendicant, desiring a sumptuous meal, even while talking of the impermanence of life, cannot stir the Tamils. To do that one should have resoluteness. He should be a foreseeing seer. He should guide the people to seek everything in the world itself and be an embodiment of his own teachings. He should not be an artist who would sell his eyes to buy a portrait. He should delight himself in the profusion of poetry. He alone who is a friend to the child, a devotee to femininity, a devil to a monster, the way to liberation and a chaser of foes, a resort for poetry and a force combining fervour and grace, can wake up the slumbering Tamil Nadu and make it walk upright.

If such a person as Bharati had not been born in Tamil Nadu, what would have happened to it is hard to guess.

Have you watched the decayed plantain regrow robustly and wondered? Similar to that, Bharati glowingly emerged on the scene that was deteriorating. We learnt from Bharati's arrival that decay was not permanent, and resurgence would soon take its place.

> "Day has dawned
> Darkness has vanished By our penance"

Tamil Nadu woke up to its resonance.

27

BHARATI REALIZED FOR HIMSELF EARLY IN LIFE THAT dawn had occurred and darkness had been dispelled. He had no ego from his prowess in writing poetry with tremendous ease. He decided to use that ability for the betterment of his country. That was the reason he could not develop an interest in school studies. Since he knew his goal early in life, he could choose his vehicle to reach it. Mind, Speech, and Action were the three elements he combined for his task. He had the courage to assert that only the Tamil language could uplift the Tamils. He dedicated himself to the cause of Tamil. It hurt him deeply when he heard someone say 'Tamil will die slowly' and he vowed to falsify it. He enlisted himself in its service unto the last.

He devoted his attention to world literature and world movements. If he found any worthy substance, then he would integrate it into Tamil. He contemplated over the stagnancy of Tamils, and found that fear was the underlying reason. Another reason was the non-cultivation of knowledge. So he endeavoured to improve knowledge and strike off fear in all ways.

He wrote poems and articles. Argued. Encouraged. He cut short the arguments of nitwits. He showed kindness to the weak and toughness to the infidels. Without losing patience, he would instruct people as if he were a schoolteacher.

Since prose was new and many Tamils were not habituated to reading, he wrote in Tamil, adopting a simple style that did not require the guidance of pundits to follow, and emphasized its practice by others, all his life. He showed interest in translating progressive works from other countries and worked to the best of his ability in that direction. He shook off meaningless and the unreasonable restrictions. The tiny seeds he sowed had grown into big plants. The droplets he sprayed swelled into floods. It is said that the hallmark of a genius is in their tireless work, and of a devotee is in doing service without complaint. Bharati was a genius and a great patriot. Is there a need to talk about his unceasing labour and action?

Bharati would dispel the doubts of others simply with his graceful presence. His charming face would make their doubts vanish. Only the corrupt and the miscreants would be frightened by him. Others would like to savour his resplendent visage. Children would be joyous when they saw his graceful face. The woman who would normally behave coyly would not do so in front of him; his face would compel her to walk with natural grace. It might not be an overstatement to say that his face guided properly during difficult times. Bharati, through known and unknown means, transmitted his ideal of 'the complete man' to the minds of the Tamils. Just as the sunrays give life to crops, Bharati made the hearts of the Tamils blossom.

At times, he would castigate Tamils directly. Immediately he would embrace them. "Can't you do it?" he would request them. He would intimidate them by saying that they would be ruined if they failed to do something. He would inject the feeling in them that there could be none equal to a Tamil, in a playful manner. He had totally changed several Tamils through his dialogues.

As if he had a premonition of his untimely death, he would never allow any opportunity to slip through. His nature was to do the job, here and now. Like Kapilar,[1] he might have concluded that another day was not our day, but the day of death. That is why his achievements loom large, despite his demise at the age of thirty-eight.

I have heard people criticise that all of Bharati's works were not gold, and they should be evaluated according to their worth. That could be true. Each of his works had carried out different functions and there was nothing to complain about. Gold should be covered with dust and kept for safety. Besides, it is only fair to offer differently according to the different needs and tastes of people. Should we stop growing neem trees since neem leaves are bitter and hence, instead of offering neem leaves to camels as their food, should we feed them with mud? If that is done we may have to eradicate the camel species. If that continues, we would have only human beings in the end. Even among them, only the infirm, who would be unable to digest food, would remain. Or only those who would adamantly refuse food. Bharati spoke and wrote with reason. It is said God had suitably measured the tail of the goat. Bharati likewise did everything after due consideration.

Do the people who are considered great perform their duties without blemish? Did not Gandhi admit to his Himalayan blunders? Should we on account of that snatch away the title of 'Mahatma' from him? Do we slap charges of murder on physicians when they fail in their duties? Sometimes living is essential; sometimes it is disgraceful. It is not advisable or meaningful to distinguish his writings as good and bad unceremoniously. Some songs are meant for children. Some, the lazy people would like. The brave will like some. Some will be like nectar to women. Lovers of music will enjoy singing some of his songs. If his works were one-dimensional, then their appeal would also be the same. Since Bharati's songs are multifaceted, they are variously appreciated.

When Bharati was born, both the Tamil language and the Tamil people were not in a good state. The Tamil language was dormant and the Tamils yearned for better, and that was how Bharati saw them. To convert them to vigour and vitality was what Bharati did with extraordinary skill. He succeeded in that.

Through his artistic talent and poetic creations, Bharati accomplished that task. He made the Tamils float on a flood of emotions. He guided people to exercise discrimination to evaluate the events in their lives. Bharati was responsible for the uprightness of the Tamils. He had great knowledge of the literature of other lands. He knew the nature of our people well. Hence, like a hybrid mango, his writings have acquired enormous taste.

You may ask about the place Bharati might occupy in world literature. Bharati was determined to identify the universal contents of mankind and embellish them. His poems cannot be viewed within the limits of 'Nationalism'. Though Bharati gave Tamils a special position, he saw them within the larger framework like other human beings. His poetry would have the same validity even if the Tamil identity given to it is taken away. He is a poet of the world. A great poet of the world. No doubt his poems would get that distinction. The way mankind is progressing now, we can say that Bharati's era will extend for a period of no less than five hundred years.

What more is there to say of his poems that are to be owned and appreciated by every citizen of the world?

Long live great Tamil!
Long live glorious Tamils!
Long live the magnificent land Bharat!
Vande Mataram!

Notes

Introduction

1. An account of Bharati coming out of *India* office as the policeman approached him with the warrant, and of the subsequent events, is found in R.A. Padmanaban, *Chitra Bharati, Documented Life Of Subramania Bharati,* Chennai, Bharati Sangam, 1980, p.50.

   S.G. Ramanujalu Naidu's account of that episode is almost the same. S.G. Ramanujalu Naidu, *Senrupona Natkal*, Edited by A.R. Venkatachalapathy, Nagercoil, Kalachuvadu Publications Pvt. Ltd, 2015, p.66.

   However, as per official records, the arrest warrant was issued in the name of M. Srinivasa Iyengar and not Bharati. Edited and published by Seeni. Viswanathan, translated by K.A. Satchidhanandham and Ira. Subbarayalu, *British Arasin Parvaiyil Bharati (1907-1909) Kalavarisaiyil Aavanap Pathivugal*, Chennai, 2018, pp.175–179.

2. The Government was considering Bharati's arrest from all possible angles. One of them was the

favourable note by Bharati that appeared in *India*, about the banned *Gaelic American* magazine that advocated independence for the Irish nation. According to the police report, Bharati was one of the thirteen readers of the magazine in Madras State. Edited and published by Seeni. Viswanathan, *British Arasin Parvaiyil Bharati (1907-1909) Kalavarisaiyil Aavanap Pathivugal*, pp.149-150.

3. Bharati left *India* even before it ceased publication. It was because he was ill-treated when the stewardship of the magazine changed hands. *Puduvaiyil Bharatiyar* by N. Nagasamy in *Bharathiyaippatri Nanpargal*, edited by R.A. Padmanaban, Kalachuvadu Publications Pvt. Ltd, 2016, p.122.
4. A.R. Venkatachalapathy, *Ezhuga Nee Pulavan*, Kalachuvadu Publications Pvt. Ltd, 2016, p.86.
5. Amartya Sen, *Tagore And India*, *The New York Review of Books*: 26 June 1997. 44.11
6. India, under the British rule, was fragmented into dominions known as 'samasthans', which were governed by the zamindars, who collected tax on behalf of the British government. Ettayapuram was the biggest samasthan in Tamil Nadu, with a few hundred villages under its Jurisdiction.
7. Compiled by C. Visvanathan, *Bharati As A Translator (A Centenary Release)*, Sivaganaga, Annam (P) Ltd, 1982.

8. M.A. Nuhman, *Bharatiyin Mozhi Sinthanaigal Oru Mozhiyiyal Nokku*, Chennai, South Vision, 1999, p.53.
9. Nirad C. Chaudhuri, *From the Archives Of A Centenarian*, Mitra and Ghosh, 1997.
10. Kanagalingam had written that a Dalit priest of Desamuthu Mariamman temple in Puducherry was also converted into a brahmin by Bharati sometime after. R. Kanagalingam, *En Gurunathar Bharatiyar*, Chapter 4.
11. Yathugiri Ammal, in her book, *Bharati Ninaivugal*, had recorded that Chellammal said that Bharati removed his poonool forever after his second daughter Sakunthala was born in 1908.
12. A.R. Venkatachalapathy first published the letter in *Mugam* magazine in February 1985. He had also noted that the publication of the letter made certain Bharati admirers unhappy. A.R. Venkatachalapathy, *Ezhuga Nee Pulavan*, p.12.
13. Karthikesu Sivathamby and A. Marx, *Bharati Maraivu Mudhal Makakavi Varai*, New Century Book House (P) Ltd. 2008, pp.74–75.
14. New India, 12 March 1915. Quoted in *Dravida Iyakka Varalaru* (1912–1921) by Murasoli Maran. Published by KAL Publications, Chennai 600004, p.192.
15. C.N. Annadurai, 'Bharati Pathai ', written in 1947, in *Peraringar Annavin Katturaigal* Part 1, Chennai, Poompuhar Pathipagam, 2008, p.688.

16. In his two-part article 'Selvam' (Wealth), Bharati gives a detailed background of what led to the Bolshevik Revolution. However, he does not favour the forceful path adopted by Lenin. He further argues that by adopting the same path of violence, the capitalists and the feudalists can overthrow the socialist state at a later date.
17. K. Kailasapathy, *Bharati Kanda Iykkaviyal* in Bharati Aaivugal, Kalachuvadu Publications Pvt Ltd, 2018.
18. M. Srinivasan Iyengar, the official editor of *India,* pleaded innocence after his arrest, and in his submission to the Magistrate mentioned that C. Subramania Bharati was paid fifty rupees every month for his editorial services, and that he himself received thirty rupees for his correspondence work, even though his name appeared as publisher, printer, and editor of *India*. Edited and published by Seeni. Viswanathan, *British Arasin Parvaiyil Bharati (1907-1909) Kalavarisaiyil Aavanap Pathivugal*, p.274.
19. Yathugiri Ammal in *Bharati Ninaivugal,* mentions Chellammal complained about Bharati not writing and sending the articles to *Swadesamitran* on time, which would have earned him money. Such things apart, it should further be borne in mind that the poor monthly income was not endemic to Tamil writers alone. Writer Tho.Mu.Si. Ragunathan shed light on the subject of the inadequate income of writers in his

biography *Pudumaipithan Varalaru,* written in 1951. While bemoaning writer Pudumaipithan's poverty, he added, 'Not only the writer in the present social condition, but the entire middle class shared the same fate.'

20. During the filming of my documentary on Subramania Bharati, I had the rarest opportunity to meet K.P. Kalyanasundaram and N. Ramasamy Iyer, both in their nineties. In their younger years, they were acquainted with Bharati. N. Ramasamy Iyer, when he was 19 years old, had occupied a portion of a house next to where Bharati lived in Thambu Chetty Street, in 1920, in Chennai.

    He narrated an interesting incident that happened when Bharati was returning home with his monthly salary of fifty rupees in a cycle rickshaw, listening to the woes of the rickshaw-puller. He gave all the money to him and reached home empty handed. Ramasamy Iyer heard about this from Chellammal, and he spotted the rickshaw-puller, to whom he gave the remainder of the sum after what he had spent.

21. Writer Pe.Su. Mani had also mentioned that Rajaji had neither brought to Gandhiji's knowledge of a song, *Vazhga nee Emman*, sung by Bharati in praise of him nor Bharati's death. To be fair to Rajaji, it should be mentioned that he wrote glowingly about Bharati as early as 1916, in Annie Besant's journal *Commonweal*,

under the caption, 'A living poet and social reformer.' After the poet's death, Rajaji translated his poems into English. These were then retranslated into Gujarati and published in Mahatma Gandhi's journal *Navjeevan* in 1929.

Pe.Su. Mani, *Bharati Pughazh Parappiya Rajaji* in *Bharatiyiyal Aaaivuk Katturaigal*. Poonkodi Pathippagam, 2001.

22. Ya. Manikandan cites Bharati's *Kovil Yaanai* – a short play he is credited with for its unearthing – as biographical evidence to conclude that the elephant attack could not have taken place just three months before his death, as is popularly understood. He dates its occurrence to nine months earlier, in 1920, the year preceding the poet's death. Ya. Manikandan, *Bharathiyin Iruthikkalam: Kovil yaanai sollum kathai*, Kalachuvadu Publications, 2014.
23. Amuthan (also mentioned by Va. Ra. as Amirutha, alias Aravamuthu Iyengar),in his book *Sri Aravinda Dharisanam*, had recorded that a member of Aurobindo's household, Nolini Kanta Gupta, gave Va. Ra. lessons in Sanskrit and Bengali.
24. Bharati in his letter, written from Puducherry, dated 3 August 1918, to his brother, C. Visvanatha Iyer, had mentioned about Va. Ra. In that Bharati had inadvertently stated that Va.Ra hailed from the Village called Thirupayanam instead of Thirupazhanam.

Bharati wrote: 'Thirupayanam V. Ramaswamy Iyengar took *Vinayagar Stotram* (Tamil book) from me for printing. It has not yet been printed. Further, he had said he would collect and send money to print *Panchali Sabatham*. I asked him to send it to my address if he managed to do this. I also asked him to expedite the work on *Vinayagar Stotram* and send its copies.' R.A. Padmanaban, Chitra Bharati, p.134.

25. 'While we were in the nascent stage, Va. Ra. had already given birth to the novel *Sundari* and reared it. It is undeniable that twenty years before our time, reformist ideals had germinated and developed in him. *Sundari* was born in 1917. It could be said that the Self-Respect Movement had just begun crawling at that time. Taking into account the ideas expressed in *Sundari,* we have to call Va. Ra. is a man of Agraharam to be wondered at.' C.N. Annadurai, *Naan Magizhchi Adaikiren*, Dravida Naadu, 18 May 1947.
26. Chittii P.K. Sundararajan and Pe.Su. Mani., *Athisaya Piravi*, Coimbatore, Vijaya Pathippagam 1999, p.56
27. Pazha. Athiyaman enumerates three instances in Va.Ra's life when he could have published Bharati's works, but did not, despite his great enthusiasm for them. He concludes that he was temperamentally unsuited for the task. Pazha. Athiyaman, *Bharati Ezhuthugal Pathippu Varalaru* in *Kidaithavarai Laabam*, Kalachuvadu Publications, 2016, pp.100–106.

28. Pa. Ramaswamy, *Va. Ra.*, Chennai, Navayuga Pirasuralayam, 1941, p.13.

Preface

1. Leo Amery served as Secretary of State for India and Burma in the Churchill War Ministry in Britain.
2. This is an allusion to Gopalakrishna Bharati's (1811-1881) *Nandanar Charithram.* Nandan, a Dalit who works as a farmhand, develops a strong spiritual desire to worship Lord Nataraja in the Chidambaram temple. His fellow slum-dwellers warn him not to develop such incompatible desires since they are not allowed to enter temples.

Chapter 1

1. Kesavan – an imaginary being. Va. Ra. introduces him as a character purely for storytelling purposes. But the storytelling instinct takes leave of him quickly. No sooner is Va. Ra. well entrenched in the events in Puducherry than the character disappears forever.
2. This reference is to a short poem by Padikasu Thambiran (16th century). The poet mentions three people who would not suffer those who erred in Tamil verse, and handed out punishments to them. One was Pillai Pandian (6th century), a scholarly King who belonged to the Pandya dynasty. Two others were the great Tamil poets Villiputhuraar (15th century) and

Ottakoothar (12th century). The punishments given to the errant Tamil practitioners varied from smiting their heads with their knuckles to beheading them. There was, however, no proof that beheading took place on account of lapses in versifications and hence it was obviously an overstatement.

3. Chellammal Bharati, in her *Bharatiyar Charithram* (Chapter 16), has mentioned that Balu was a man with a well-built physique, and was one of the disciples that Bharati sent to hamlets to provide education to Dalits.

Chapter 3

1. Subramania Siva, Bharati, and V.O. Chidambaram Pillai were often seen as the triumvirate in their opposition to British rule of India, and were united by their devotion to Bal Gangadhar Tilak. Siva was a fiery orator and writer. Bharati's writings, including *Chinna Sankaran Kathai,* were published in Siva's journal *Gnana Banu*. After Bharati's death, Siva conducted his first memorial meeting.
2. Parali. Su. Nellaiyappar (1889–1950) was a freedom fighter and the editor of the magazine *Lokopakari.* He was closely associated with V.O. Chidambaram Pillai. Bharati affectionately called him 'Thambi', meaning 'younger brother'. He dared to publish Bharati's poems when Bharati was alive. R.A. Padmanaban, *Chitra Bharati*, p.126.

3. During Bharati's lifetime, Ettayapuram Samasthan was ruled by two zamindars. Raja Maharaja Venkatesura Ettappa Naicker was the one that the young Bharati associated with. The interesting anecdotes shared by Bharati with Va. Ra. were about him. He appeared as Ramasamy Kavundar in Bharati's *roman à clef* novella *Chinna Sankaran Kathai.* Thatha Venkatesura Ettappa Naicker, who succeeded him, was approached for financial assistance by Bharati in his later years. Bharati also volunteered to rewrite the ancestry of Ettayapuram rulers for him. The poet's entreaties brought nothing. However, when Bharati Manimandapam was built in Ettayapuram in 1948, the same ruler donated the land for its building.

Chapter 4

1. Chinnasamy Iyer married Valliammal two and a half years after the death of Lakshmi Ammal, his first wife and Bharati's mother. Lakshmi, the daughter, and Viswanatha Iyer, the son, were born of that marriage.
2. Lekiyam is an electuary prepared from herbs for medicinal purposes. However, the aforementioned *pooranathi lekiyam*, recommended by the Raja, was actually a narcotic to boost virility and not to stimulate digestion. (Ref. Tamil Lexicon. University of Madras, 1982, Vol. 5, Part 1, p.2846). It is clear that the Raja wanted to play pranks on him. From the accounts

given of the Raja, one cannot of course infer anything else. Va. Ra. has not given Bharati's account of it; in his happy mood that would have thrown more light on its specific effects on Bharati.

Chapter 5

1. Koolappa Nayak, a chieftain, fell in love with a tribal girl named Navaratnamalai. Their intimate relationship was graphically narrated by Supradeepa Kavirayar. The 'adult' work written in the 17th century was privately read and enjoyed.
2. G. Subramania Iyer (1855–1916) was among the principal figures of the early freedom movement in South India, and a journalist with a fierce writing style. He was one of the founders of the English newspaper *The Hindu* in 1878 and founded the Tamil Newspaper *Swadesamitran* in 1882. Since Iyer was solely responsible for inducting Bharati into journalism, Bharati was greatly indebted to him. He had progressive ideas on women and wanted abolition of untouchability. He also insisted that Tamils should use only Tamil among themselves as the language for communication, all of which greatly influenced Bharati. Subramania Iyer also appears as a fictional character in Bharati's short novel *Chandrikaiyin Kathai* (Story of Chandrikai), where he gives active guidance to a widow on her remarriage proposal.

Chapter 6

1. The Mandayam family invested, at the behest of Bharati, several thousand rupees in V.O. Chidambaram Pillai's doomed patriotic venture, the Swadeshi Shipping Company. *Bharati Pudaiyal Perunthiratu* – compiled by R.A. Padmanaban, Vanathi Pathippagam, 1982, p.352.

Chapter 7

1. *Puthiya Aathichudi* i.e. New Aathichudi. Originally, Aathichudi poems were written by the poet Avvai, supposedly belonging to the period of 12th century. They are a set of adages, each not exceeding three words, and organised in alphabetical order. Bharati reworked them in *Puthiya Aathichudi,* infusing his ideas on morality.

Chapter 8

1. Sardar Ajit Singh (1881–1947) was a freedom fighter. He shot to prominence by opposing the water cess tax levied against farmers, which was known as the Punjab Colonisation Act (Amendment) 1906. He was deported to Mandalay in Burma in 1907. He participated in the Surat Congress meeting. Bharati had given a glowing account of his activities. Subramania Bharati, *Engal Congress Yathirai* in *Bharati Pudaiyal Perunthiratu* –

Compiled by R. A. Padmanaban, pp.514–518.

2. Valluvar (aka Tiruvalluvar), the revered ancient Tamil poet, wrote Tirukural in 1,330 couplets.
3. Saigon Chinnaiah was drawn to the Indian Freedom struggle. He was close to Bharati and sent copies of *India* to British India secretly. He started a weekly magazine called *Desa Sevakan* in 1922 in Puducherry that didn't hesitate to criticise the wrongdoings of the French India government. S. Thillaivanam, *Puducherry Manilam Varalarum Panpadum*, Puducherry, Sivasakthi Pathippagam. 2007, p.170.

Chapter 9

1. G. S. Khaparde (1854–1938) was a lawyer and a political activist. Bharati had mentioned him as one of those who had shielded Bal Gangadhar Tilak from the attacks by moderates in the Congress meeting that ended up in a melee in Surat in 1907. Subramania Bharati, *Engal Congress Yathirai* in *Bharati Pudaiyal Perunthiratu* – compiled by R. A. Padmanaban, p.530.

Chapter 10

1. Pushcart is 'Pousse-Pousse' in French. A pushcart is kept on display at Puducherry Museum.

Chapter 13

1. This line is from Stanza 64 of the 7th century-Saint–Poet Andal's *Nachiyar Thirumozhi*. One of the twelve Azhvars, her most well-known work is *Thiruppavai*.
2. Thayumanavar was an 18th century Tamil spiritual poet. Bharati had written a poem on him, praising that he would live as long as the Tamil language itself.

Chapter 14

1. Robert William d'EsCourt Ashe was the Acting Collector of the British Raj. He was shot dead by freedom fighter, Vanchinathan, on 17 June 1911 at Maniyachchi Railway Station for his role in the torture of Congress leader V.O. Chidambaram Pillai in prison. The railway station is renamed Vanchi Maniyachchi Railway Station in honour of the freedom fighter.

Chapter 19

1. Khyal is a Hindustani musical genre. In khyal, the lines are repeated over and over again for musical effect. Since he was sarcastic about 'Swadeshis', Bharati might have meant that they were stagnating and not moving forward due to their fear or they were vacuously amusing themselves by singing.

Chapter 20

1. In Chapter 3, Va. Ra. writes that the story *Chinna Sankaran Kathai* was originally 30 chapters long. We would never know how many chapters there were in Bharati's manuscript, which has been lost forever. When the rewritten story was published as a book in 1953, it had only four chapters. Bharati wrote the story under the pseudonym Savitri. *Kala Varisai Paduthappatta Bharati Padaippugal*, published by Seeni. Viswanathan, 2006, p.297

Chapter 21

1. This is a reference to how the Gopikas, the consorts of Krishna, responded to Bhagavatham by shouting back, 'Govinda, Govinda' when they were asked to fix their attention on Govinda.

Chapter 22

1. Maha Vaidyanatha lyer (1884–1893) was a talented carnatic music Tamil composer. Madurai Pushpavanam lyer (1885–1917) was a carnatic vocalist known for his melodious voice.

Chapter 23

1. These lines are from a poem by the Tamil poet, Avvai. The poem uses the pillar under heavy burden as an

analogy to imply that those who stood by the King would rather die in war than give up.

2. The infamous Rowlatt Act of 1919, based on the report of Justice Rowlatt, empowered the British government to detain anyone who opposed it for a period of two years without a warrant. Mahatma Gandhi came to Chennai in March 1919 and stayed at Rajaji's house. The leaders met there for the first time. During their stay on the night of 18 March 1919, Gandhi was deeply worried by the Act and became sleepless. He decided then to begin a countrywide protest. Gandhi met Rajaji in March, and not in February. Again, Gandhi had not yet chosen Chennai to launch his agitation against Rowlatt Act from. The idea was only born there, as he had said in his own words: "In that twilight condition, between sleep and consciousness, when suddenly the idea broke upon me". Hence the order of events is not as given by Va. Ra.

Chapter 25

1. "Oliver Goldsmith, a poet, naturalist, and historian, who left scarcely any style of writing untouched, and touched nothing that he did not adorn." Dr. Johnson's epitaph for Oliver Goldsmith.

Chapter 26

1. Therukoothu, a traditional folk theatre of Tamil Nadu.

Chapter 27

1. Va. Ra. refers to the lines from Bharati's poem 'Sri Kapilar Agaval'.

Timeline of Important Events in Bharati's Life

1882	11 December. C. Subramanian is born to parents Chinnasamy Iyer and Lakshmi Ammal in Ettayapuram, Tirunelveli District.
1887	Lakshmi Ammal dies.
1893	Sivagnana Yogi confers the title 'Bharati' on Chinnasamy Subramanian at the Ettayapuram court.
1895	Bharati is admitted to Hindu College, Tirunelveli.
1897	27 June. Bharati marries Chellammal, aged seven.
1898	Chinnasamy Iyer dies. Bharati leaves to Benares to live with his aunt Kuppammal.
1900	Bharati passes Allahabad University Examination.
1903	On the invitation of Ettayapuram zamindar, Bharati returns to Ettayapuram from Benares.

1904

In July his poem *Thanimaiyirakkam* (a Sonnet of Solitude) appears in *Vivekabanu* as Bharati's first published work. From 1 August to 10 November he works as a Tamil teacher in Madurai Sethupathy High School in Madurai. In November, Bharati joins *Swadesamitran* in Chennai at the invitation of its editor G.Subramania Iyer.

1905

Thangammal, Bharati's first daughter is born. Bharati works simultaneously in *Chakravarthini*, a new magazine started exclusively for women.

1906

September. Bharati joins *India* weekly as its unofficial editor. His highly critical writings of the British rule in India feature in it.

1907

Bharati participates in the Congress meeting held in Surat.

1908 – 1918: A highly eventful decade in Bharati's life; to avoid arrest from the British government he leaves for Puduchery in 1908 and remains there until 1918; His second daughter Sakunthala is born in 1908 and the family is brought to Puduchery; Bharati writes and works in varying capacities in several magazines including *Vijaya, Bala Bharata, Karmayogi* and *India* which is republished; Writes three of his most important works- *Kuyil Pattu, Kannan Pattu* and *Panchali Sabatham*; When he finally leaves Puduchery he is arrested and detained in Cuddalore Sub Jail from 24 November 1918 to 14 December 1918 for a period of twenty four days.

1919: Stays in Kadayam. Meets M. K. Gandhi in Chennai.

1920: Bharati writes to many seeking financial help to publish his collected works. Relocates to Chennai with family. Joins *Swadesamitran* as an assistant editor.

1921: Dies after a brief illness on 12 September.

Bharati's Works in English

Agni and other poems and translations of essays and other prose fragments by C. Subramania Bharati – Edited by C. Visvanatha Ayyar, Novel Art Printers, 1980.

Bharati Karuvoolam – Hindu Nalithalil Bharatiyin Eluthugal Edited by A.R. Venkatachalapathy, Kalachuvadu Publications Pvt Ltd, 2008. The book contains Bharati's letters in English written to 'The Hindu' newspaper along with their Tamil translations and notes by the editor.

C. Subramania Bharati – The Coming Age. Collected English writings. Edited by Mira. T. Sundara Rajan, Penguin, 2021.

Recommended Reading

Bharati's works in English translation by others:

Poems of Subramania Bharati, translated by Prema Nandakumar, Sahitya Akademi, 1982.

Bharati Patalkal, translated by T.N. Ramachandran and others, Thanjavur University, 1989.

Subramania Bharati Volume 1. Poems. Volume 2. Essays and Stories. Edited by Sirpi Balasubramaniam. Published by Sahitya Akademi, 2016.

Index

CASTE AWAY: PERSPECTIVES ON CASTE-EQUALITY STRUGGLES IN TAMIL NADU

NA. VANAMAMALAI

Translated and with an introduction by JOSHUA GNANASELVAN

NATIONALIZED TAMIL BOOKS IN TRANSLATION SERIES

A pithy and momentous collection of essays on caste-equality struggles in Tamil Nadu by scholar and social activist Na. Vanamamalai

Offering a meticulous exploration of Tamil Nadu's intricate caste dynamics, Na. Vanamamalai's pivotal work unveils the endeavours of 'lower-caste' communities in challenging established hierarchies. It spans the Chola dynasty to the early part of the twentieth century. Through extensive research and insightful analysis, the renowned scholar elucidates how certain communities strategically appropriated the *varna* system, elevating their social status. Drawing on various source texts – historical documents, verses by socially committed ascetics, court judgments – the work demonstrates how the Chola kings tactically offered concessions to different caste clusters, thereby navigating a delicate balance between benefits and exploitation.

Caste Away compellingly argues that caste-based conflicts were fundamentally manifestations of class antagonisms, and challenges conventional interpretations, showing how the pursuit of caste equality was aimed not at creating an egalitarian society but at elevating the social standing of specific castes.